THE FILMS OF AMOS GITAI

THE FILMS OF AMOS GITAI
A MONTAGE

EDITED BY **PAUL WILLEMEN**

BFI PUBLISHING

First published in 1993 by the
British Film Institute
21 Stephen Street
London W1P 1PL

The British Film Institute exists to encourage the development of film, television and video in the United Kingdom, and to promote knowledge, understanding and enjoyment of the culture of the moving image.
Its activities include the National Film and Television Archive; the National Film Theatre; the Museum of the Moving Image; the London Film Festival; the production and distribution of film and video; funding and support for regional activities; Library and Information Services; Stills, Posters and Designs; Research; Publishing and Education; and the monthly *Sight and Sound* magazine.

Copyright © The British Film Institute
Introductions and editorial matter
© Paul Willemen
All previously published material
© original source
Previously unpublished material
© author 1993

Design by Stella Crew, 2D Design

Cover Still by Lea Ando

British Library Cataloguing-in-Publication Data.
A catalogue for this book is available from the British Library

ISBN 0-85170-416-6

Printed in Great Britain by
The Trinity Press,
Worcester

An African philosophy argues that man's most terrible enemy is disease. Or, perhaps, not disease but rather death. But when you give it another thought, you understand that the true fatal enemy of humankind is not disease, nor is it death, but ignorance. Ignorance is the worst of evils for humanity. There is no one more ignorant than the one who never stepped outside his own house. Exile is a school, the great school of life. Exile cures the wounds of ignorance and incarnates tolerance.

Sotigui Kouyaté

CONTENTS

PREFACE 1
Paul Willemen

PART I ESSAYS

BANGKOK-BAHRAIN-BERLIN-JERUSALEM 5
Paul Willemen
GITAI THE NOMADIC IMAGE 16
Alberto Farassino
THE ROAD TO JERUSALEM 19
Mikhail Iampolski
AN ARCHITECTONICS OF RESPONSIBILITY 24
Irma Klein
A VIEW FROM WITHIN 37
Taline Voskeritchian
BROKEN DREAMS – Three Gitai Films
PINEAPPLE, ESTHER AND BERLIN-JERUSALEM 42
Asish Rajadhyaksha

PART II THE FILMS

BAIT 45
  Serge Daney, Julian Petley, Mikael Harsgor, Stuart Klawans
WADI 46
  Angelika Kettelhack, Susan Barrowclough
FIELD DIARY 48
  Selim Nassib, Yann Lardeau, Julian Petley
ANANAS 52
  David Lusted
BANGKOK BAHRAIN 54
  Michael Eaton
ESTHER 56
  Richard Ingersoll, Rachel Neeman, Tamar Meroz
BERLIN-JERUSALEM 62
  Philippe Garrel
GOLEM-L'ESPRIT DE L'EXIL 64
  Markus and Simon Stockhausen, Marco Melani
METAMORFOSI DI UNA MELODIA 68
  Edoardo Bruno

PART III
GITAI ON GITAI 71

PART IV
ALEKAN ON GITAI 99

PART V
BIO-FILMOGRAPHY 107

Amos Gitai and Bernado Bertolucci on the set of *Golem – The Spirit of Exile*

PREFACE

Paul Willemen

Philippe Garrel, one of France's most challenging film authors, opened a brief article about Amos Gitai in *Libération* simply stating 'Amos is a poet'. Bernardo Bertolucci, after acting the role of a bailiff in Gitai's *Golem-L'Esprit de l'exil* (1992), elaborated: 'Was Cocteau thinking of Amos Gitai when he said that a camera can be a wonderful and dangerous weapon in the hands of a poet? A feeling of danger was rising in the courtyard where we were shooting. Maybe this is what one feels all the time, the other side of the camera, together with the blind pleasure of acting without knowing anything. It's intense and powerful. I find the film hypnotic.' And commenting on Gitai's overall approach to the cinema, the great Yussef Shahine said, in 1985: 'Gitai is such a courageous person that I would be surprised if he weren't admired throughout the world. He is exceedingly courageous. Gitai dared. He dares to go very, very far. For me, it is the duty of a cineaste to dare. If you don't, what is it you want your films to say? It is our duty to pass on to others everything we know. To generations coming after us, in order to find a way of understanding, at last, this world which is cut up by borders, and stupidity, and religions and colours. It is insane.'

And yet, the innovative cinematic work of Amos Gitai is best known in Britain only to viewers of Channel 4 Television's few genuinely exploratory programmes and to people who attend film festivals. In the USA, his films are often shown in festivals and on special occasions such as retrospectives devoted specifically to his work. Rarely have his films received the exposure they deserve in cinemas, although some of his features have been programmed in art-house cinemas in continental Europe. In this respect, Gitai's cinema is analogous to the work of, for instance, Jean-Marie Straub and Danielle Huillet. Films that are not regularly programmed in cinemas are liable to be described as appealing only to minority audiences. There is some truth to that description, but it tends to overlook two important questions. Firstly, why should films not be made for minority audiences? Secondly, if we abandon short term economics and take a longer view, the audiences accumulated by Gitai's work over a period of years easily tops that of many 'mainstream' directors simply because its quality demands, and receives, repeated attention.

There is, however, a downside to the lack of consistent screenings in cinemas offset by repeated screenings on television. Since the bulk of television criticism in Britain and in the US has just about reached the stage film criticism had achieved in the 1920s and 30s (superficial consumer guidance in the daily press and extensive gossip devoted to the industry's mass consumer items and personalities) the discussion of Gitai's work has been restricted to specialised, relatively small circulation journals. The odd special feature in *The Village Voice* merely confirms that rule. On the contrary, in France and in Italy, the quality press devotes full-page features to Gitai's films while still in production even though in those countries too his films are considered to be part of a minority culture. This may say a great deal about different national cultures' interest in and ability to sustain film cultures as well as about the way different countries perceive the complex relationships between minority and mainstream cultures. Nevertheless, the fact that most people see Gitai's films via television means that the kind of critical discourse which explores the coherence and extends the productivity of Gitai's approach to the cinema remains sporadic.

This montage of essays and interviews aims to present Gitai's work as a coherent and lucid cinematic investigation of some of the most important issues in contemporary culture. The films engage directly with questions of physical displacement in terms of exile and migration and of discursive displacement in terms of the life of myths and legends in apparently thoroughly technicised societies. In addition, the related motifs of memory and history, of short term and long term (over)determinations at work within the here and now are brought into focus. As such, Gitai's work, though often starting from the Jewish diaspora, must also be seen as addressing diasporic phenomena in general. Metaphorically speaking, we could say that Gitai has found a way of filming borders: borders between countries, borders within countries, between and within people, in space and in time. Gitai often resorts to two images to describe this filming of borders. The first one is that of the archaeologist who explores layers of history vertically. The second one is that of the editor who works by way of juxtapositions on the linear, horizontal axis. The result is a kind of three-dimensional perspective which, in his interviews, is conveyed by means of architectural similes and, in his shooting style, by means of sequence shots taken with a very mobile camera gliding through spaces sculpted with light (natural light in the documentaries, Henri Alekan's dramatic light sculptures in the features).

The most pertinent conflicts in Gitai's films are not really between people. Those conflicts are presented as eminently avoidable even though they keep occurring with distressingly lethal regularity. The real conflicts are between time and space, that is to say, between the temporalities at work within and imposed upon geographical spaces. Whereas institutions such as governments, corporations, armies and so on seek to homogenise and synchronise life on the terrains they control, people, as carriers of memories and dreams, must, if they are to remain truly alive, resist the Procrustean rigours of homogeneity and synchronicity (or 'Gleichschaltung', as the Nazi programme put it). This inevitably produces a lack of fit between, on the one hand, the regulatory intentions of institutions and, on the other hand, both the people who enforce and the people who resist those regulatory pressures. Cases in point are for instance the soldiers in *Field Diary* who feel unhappy in their allotted role as occupiers or the Jewish militants in *Berlin-Jerusalem* who by seeking to escape from oppression, produce it. Each, by seeking to realise their dreams not only ends up destroying the dreams of others but also their own. Gitai's cinema constitutes a search for an escape from this tragically vicious circle, not by advocating an escape from history but the contrary: by advocating a critical awareness of this fundamental social contradiction. A critical awareness of the process is the first step towards alleviating its most negative effects for ourselves and for others at the same time. In addition, learning to live with the contradiction means acknowledging that we desire simultaneously two mutually exclusive things, something Gitai stated, characteristically, by quoting an ancient sage: 'Gershem Sholem quotes a rabbi of the 13th century, Rabbi de la Rena, who, when asked about the Messiah, answers "May he come, but I don't want to see him." So there is the desire to achieve utopia, but also the resistance against it. Maybe this expresses the profound understanding that utopias are there as a sense of direction but not as something to be actualised.'

All the essays in the first part of this book, with the exception of Taline Voskeritchian's contribution, were written especially for this collection. They address the main aspects of Gitai's films, features as well as documentaries, from a variety of cultural and political perspectives. The second part contains essays and extracts from reviews devoted to Gitai's best known (to date) films. The book closes with a complete filmography annotated, where appropriate, with the film-maker's comments describing the project. In between, there are brief sections presenting extracts from interviews and statements where Gitai talks about more general aspects of his work and preoccupations.

The guiding principle underpinning the selections is mainly a negative one: the avoidance of too much repetition. The chosen extracts do not necessarily convey a value judgment on the essay or the review from which they were taken. As editor of the book, I have acted rather like a film editor juxtaposing fragments in the hope of achieving an overall structure that does justice to Amos Gitai's three-dimensional world, making room for a plurality of voices which overlap and diverge. In this way, I hoped to construct a montage of discourses rather like Gitai constructs his films, offering the reader-viewer materials to think with, gently challenging the reader-viewer to displace him/herself both intellectually and geographically, all the better to see the borders and the shapes of our present predicament.

Special thanks are due to all those who have worked with Amos Gitai and who have written about his work. In particular, I gratefully acknowledge the work of interviewers such as Stephan Levine, Simon Mizrahi and all those who elicited the replies and the remarks by Amos Gitai which have been quoted and the publications which printed the interviews (references have been provided only when the questions are quoted as well); the generosity of the authors who wrote a new essay for this publication; the help of John Stewart and Alberto Farassino, who published the books on which the present work is based; Ilona Halberstadt, Judith Landry, Eléonore Feneux of AGAV Films; Roma Gibson; Stella Crew and Mike Leedham of 2D Design; and Rivka Markovitzky. However, the most important contribution to this book was made by the Mostra Internazionale of Rimini directed by Alberto Farassino.

PART I
ESSAYS

BANGKOK-BAHRAIN-BERLIN-JERUSALEM

Paul Willemen

Rephrasing Ricoeur and Foucault in one of the most illuminating essays of the 80s about the dynamics at work in Euro-American cultures, Andreas Huyssen wrote:

> There is a growing awareness that other cultures, especially non-European and Non-Western cultures, must be met by means other than conquest or domination. This awareness will have to translate into a type of intellectual work different from that of the modernist intellectual who typically spoke with the confidence of standing at the cutting edge of time and of being able to speak for others. Foucault's notion of the local and the specific intellectual of opposed to the 'universal' intellectual of modernity may provide a way out of the dilemma of being locked into our own culture and traditions while simultaneously recognising their limitations. ('Mapping the postmodern' in *New German Critique*, no. 33, 1984.)

This quotation is perhaps too grandiose a way of opening a modest discussion of a few points triggered by viewings of Amos Gitai's extraordinary films, and particularly of his documentary *Bangkok-Bahrain* (1984) concerning the physical exploitation of Thai people's bodies, male and female, by different kinds of imperialisms (US, Europe, Arab). However, it allows me to begin by drawing attention to an increasingly pressing problem which faces cultural critics today: the fact that theory and criticism are intellectual practices very much tied to specific historical moments and geographical locations. In other words, what I feel energised enough to try to theorise, the issues I feel compelled to address and the terms in which I address them, are determined significantly by the situation in which I live and work. In my case, this is contemporary Britain. While this is a readily acknowledged truism for most intellectuals, it is also something rarely taken into account in the actual formulation of our work.

Working in Britain, there is no escaping the need to engage with cultural heterogeneity, since the most vital aspects of cultural life here are to be found in the British Afro-Caribbean and British-Asian sectors (the plural is necessary because, as the compound terms suggest, the sectors themselves do not constitute homogeneous terrains). The cultural practices of Asian countries are also emerging as powerful challenges, although their impact, except for that of the Islamic reactionaries aligned (for whatever reasons) with the Iranian government, still seems less forceful.

In such a context it is, perhaps, not surprising that intellectuals faced with the need to meet other cultures in ways other than through conquest or domination, are tempted to succumb to a kind of traumatic aphasia. In England, especially, intellectuals have played very murky roles in history and the infamy of their politics has been used as a stick to beat all intellectual work without exception. This has made the life of the left intelligentsia in UKania, to borrow Tom Nairn's apt term for the British Isles, very difficult at the best of times. Over the last decade or so, throughout the 80s, the main response of those left intellectuals active in the 70s has been to try to efface themselves altogether, to abdicate the function and responsibilities of intellectual work. They are traumatised by the overwhelming atmosphere of anti-intellectualism, combined with the belated realisation of the contradictions inherent in the very position of being simultaneously an intellectual and on the left – that is, people who may have access to cinematic production, to video and to television, publishing, lecture platforms, and so on, but who are not aligned with the powers which control and occupy, in the military sense of the term, those media sites.

Whereas in the 1960s and 1970s there still existed a kind of confidence of speaking from the cutting edge of changing times and of cultural development in the formulation of theories of cultural struggles, that confidence, fortunately, has evaporated. Unfortunately, however, it left a vacuum in its wake as many of the intellectuals concerned tried to prosper, or were forced to find a way of surviving in the suffocating 80s. Now, the vast majority of British film and video makers, as well as the cultural critics, are either desperately trying to become invisible or to turn their coats and present themselves as celebrants of the consumer cultures associated with the triumph of finance capitalism in the western heartlands. Examples of these trends can be found in Sean Cubitt's breathless ode to the adman's mental universe, *Timeshift* (London: Routledge, 1991) and in television programmes like *The Media Show* (Channel Four Television, 1987-91). For examples of intellectuals craving invisibility, see the numerous 'community' videos, often described as films, produced throughout UKania.

Those opting for invisibility tend to delude themselves into believing that they function merely as channels for others to speak through, those others being 'the oppressed', or some such category. Any suggestion that intellectuals have a responsibility, by virtue of their education and social position, to exercise their intellectual skills and knowledges in order to analyse the dynamics at work in their social formation, is dismissed as 'elitist'. Instead, they stand aside to clear the way for the voices of the particular group with which they have chosen to identify. At least, that is the fantasy. In fact, they do not stand aside at all, but occupy the media space with repeated calls for intellectuals to submit to the injunction that their skills are to be discarded in favour of expressions emanating from an allegedly popular consciousness, as if that consciousness were not already deeply marked by the discourses and products of the media industries in the first place.

The vast majority of those who might be left intellectuals no longer speak in that capacity. No doubt, there are some benefits to this stance: the voices coming through as a result are indeed often more interesting and intellectually astute than whatever the traumatised film and video makers might have come up with themselves. The negative effect, however, is more crippling: an almost terroristic imposition of the crudest types of populism takes the place of intellectual analysis. In England today (although there are some faint signs of a possible change) a malevolently paranoid anti-intellectualism seeks to stifle any critical intellectual work, especially work critical of consumer cultures (see, for instance, Valerie Walkerdine's contribution to *Formations of Fantasy*, London: Methuen, 1986) while journals, papers and television are teeming with celebrants of shopping and devotees of the short-term, rapid turnover (cultural) investment strategy characteristic of contemporary finance capital.

The brutalising effects of this development are particularly noticeable in the area of documentary film-making, where many community and other 'left' media practitioners consider it almost a crime for a film-maker to assume responsibility for his or her discourse and to be seen to be shaping an analytical discourse in the form of a film or a television programme. A case in point is the negative reaction from the liberal and left intelligentsia to the four-part film, *Nicaragua* (1985), shown on Channel 4 and made by the best documentary film-maker working in Britain today, Marc Karlin. What seemed to be most objectionable was the film-maker's inclusion in the films of an exploration of the issues involved in the representation of Nicaragua, filmically or photographically, by non-Nicaraguans. Karlin had committed the cardinal sin of questioning the terms in which we produce and consume images.

It is because of the damaging effects of these developments that I want to turn to the work of the Israeli film-maker Amos Gitai, who is elaborating, alongside his work in fiction, a kind of essayistic film-making particularly relevant to us in Europe (but elsewhere also) in the late 20th century.

In a situation in which television has become virtually the only source of money, as well as providing the main channels of exhibition for film, different registers of audiovisual discourse are emerging with different implications as to the mode of attention they invite and require. Gitai's films are made with television money and mostly transmitted via television, but they nevertheless require a cinematic mode of attention. That is to say, they require a considerable amount of concentration over extended periods of time, close attention being paid to editing patterns, camera movements, composition in depth and lighting patterns.

Traditionally, editing has been used and discussed as a way of limiting ambiguity, as a way of making sure that viewers follow and receive as exclusively as possible the sense which film-makers want the viewers to receive. In other words, editing is used primarily to impose, as far as this is possible, a reading. More recently, in music-television and other types of television advertising, editing has been subordinated to the music track and is used to enjoin people to 'stop making sense' and to absorb and live by 'moods'. Both the imposition and the prevention of sense-making illustrate the manipulatively authoritarian aspect of editing which was given one of its most sophisticated formulations in Eisenstein's early writings and in his theory of montage. The issue of the implicit authoritarianism of editing was the bone of contention between, for instance, Eisenstein and Bazin, the latter arguing for Christian Democratic sequence shots and deep-focus compositions. Although it is true that editing is a manipulative technique staking out the path the reader/viewer is supposed to follow, the matter is slightly more complex, as Eisenstein himself acknowledged in his discussions of colour and frame composition. The point is that in cinema a multiplicity of codes operates to generate meaning, of which the cuts propelling viewers from one bundle of meanings to another is perhaps the main, but not the only one. Moreover, these cuts acquire meaning only in relation to the disposition, the montage, of signifying elements within the shots, so that it might be more accurate, as far as cinema is concerned anyway, to talk of the orchestration of meanings.

Again, the current and increasingly dominant forms of television seek to reduce the complexity of this orchestration by reducing the pertinent field of vision, and therefore of potential meanings, almost exclusively to the human face and torso. The result is the near total loss of any notion of cinema, as television-derived aesthetics swamp all forms of audiovisual discourse: actorial 'character' drama narrated in close shots of advertising-inspired kitschy showiness are the norm. Engagement with a sense of place or time has to make way for an exclusive focus on quirky individuals. Time and again, we are forced to detour through an identification with some allegedly interesting character or person if we are to be granted access to the socio-cultural forces shaping the world in which we live, as we are stuck with our noses up against samples of warm and wonderful humanity emoting in close-up.

Gitai's films, together with those of a number of other prominent but still fairly unfamiliar film-makers such as Chantal Akerman, Ousmane Sembene, Ritwik Ghatak and David and Judith McDougall, deploy a type of orchestration of meaning not often discussed but important for the artistic as well as the intellectual value of the medium. In Gitai's films, as in Marc Karlin's, the authorial voice is neither authoritarian nor effaced. Instead, the films are marked by a strategy of address that tries to mobilise meanings rather than impose them. It works with the cultural and the political knowledges assumed to be present in the viewer, calling on non-automatic, non-normative ways of deciphering one's environment. The process of meaning production is activated by working with, as well as upon, the viewer's skills and knowledge, trying to re-articulate them into improved, more complex and more comprehensive ways of making sense of and with the material presented. The viewer is not manipulated, and neither is he or she left to his/her 'own' devices, which invariably are the devices made available and strenuously advocated by and in the daily press and by television's cultural functionaries. Instead, a kind of dialogue is set up between the film-maker and viewer in which the film-maker proposes a way of making sense but simultaneously invites critical attention to the way this is done, regularly pausing to allow the reader/viewer to check the proceedings.

This in-between way of proceeding – in-between intellectual and mood manipulation – is rather difficult to define or even to describe. An example may help to clarify the point. Think of a medium long shot held for a considerable length of time, with or without camera movement, such as a sequence shot. During the viewing of such a shot, complex changes occur in our mode of attention to what is depicted as we begin to take in aspects of the scene normally overlooked (that is, aspects of the scene we have been dis-habituated from attending to), such as background details, changes of light, ambient sounds, landscape details, and so on. The scene comes alive as our relation to what we see is activated as a significant component of our viewing experience. The cognitive value of the scene changes as we work with the whole range of the materials on offer.

Often, the effect of such a scene or of a sequence shot will be to allow the characters in it (if there are any) to begin functioning 'in context', as we begin to become aware of the environment within which the character operates and which, precisely because we are given the opportunity to attend to the environmental details, co-determines in important ways the nature and status of that character itself. In such a sequence, individuals are allowed to be seen as social beings existing within, and marked by, very specific geo-social circumstances. We are no longer forced to detour our attention through 'identification' with a character in order to gain access to the fiction or to the signified world. The emotional relation between character and viewer is no longer at the centre of the picture. Instead, the relation between a character and its context, presented perhaps not as all-determining but at least as very significant, becomes the focus of attention. The emotive realism banking on character identification has thus been bypassed and its equally restrictive obverse, the foregrounding of the processes of enunciation, is thus avoided as well. In other words, this strategy of address is neither realist nor modernist in the traditional senses of those terms in cultural theory.

Instead of requiring us to submit to the inexorably sequenced bits of meaning strung together fast enough to disallow any attention to the textures and to the actual substance of the meanings and moods we are asked to undergo, this type of orchestration relies on complex interactions, spread over time, between a scene and its viewer. One could almost call it dialogic if that term had not been rendered meaningless by its fashionable over-and misuse. In the spaces where we notice the processes of construction, the film-maker says 'I' and addresses us as interlocutors as well as witnesses. The mark of enunciation are there, as they are in conventional modernism, but contrary to the modernist styles, they are subordinated to the essayistic discourse and the referential argument that discourse is conducting. In this sense, Gitai's films present a discourse about a topic in the form of an argument, rather than an order, addressed to us. The film does not shrivel into empty rhetoric if we disagree with aspects of the argument: we can still work with the materials presented in order to formulate other arguments, to make other kinds of 'sense'. Moreover, the argument presented is embedded in such richly and complexly detailed sets of relations deployed at a pace that allows for contemplation and reflection, that the authorial voice itself is somewhat displaced. It is no longer a case of the author, with or without the use of voice-over narration, marshalling images and sounds to buttress his or her argument, but rather of the presentation of pertinent (along with ancillary) facets of a set of interconnected issues about which the authorial voice offers a by no means continuously clear-cut position. The author can thus assume full responsibility for the discourse constructed without having to hide behind either a bogus neutrality (as in, for example, Fred Wiseman's documentaries) or the pyrotechnics of flashy enunciation strategies (as in some films of Godard, for example), these being the two best-known alternatives to the routinely authoritarian practices of 'social concern' films. Gitai provides a nudging, essentially friendly kind of discourse, acknowledging the presence alongside him of the viewer and assuming a shared interest in the attempt to understand, to make sense of the particular social processes the film is about.

After making *Ananas* (1983), a documentary using one particular commodity to trace relations of exploitation, imperialism and resistance in the era of transnational capitalism, Gitai made *Bangkok-Bahrain* (1984) about the exploitation of Thai men and women. He shows and discusses the dislocations brought about in Thailand by the US attack on Vietnam and then goes on to discuss the use of female and male Thai bodies, the former in the Bangkok sex-tourism industry, the latter in the Middle Eastern construction industry, which has its own brand of pimps in the form of traffickers in migrant labour. Up to this point, the film proceeds with fairly long, meandering shots, sometimes with static camera as we listen to someone's story. The camera has remained primarily observational, in the position of a visitor who is not always welcome and who tactfully keeps his distance.

Then we encounter an extraordinary sequence shot. It starts with a televisual framing of a trafficker seated behind a desk as he is interviewed on camera. He is lit in the standard television manner in medium close-up as he replies to some questions about his unsavoury job. Then, as the film-maker asks a question referring to a previous conversation not shown in the film, the camera hesitantly but doggedly pans right and reveals the man's wife, sitting in the corner of the room, not properly lit at all and obviously expecting to remain out of the frame. Pinned to the wall by the camera movement, she responds to the question. But suddenly, the whole situation has been changed by this obvious infringement by the film-maker of an agreement that must have been made prior to filming: the agreement not to film her, demonstrated by the absence of professional lighting.

To debate whether this agreement was made explicitly or not is beside the point, since the initial set-up and the lights make it clear that she was in a no-film area. The pan, resulting in the 'badly lit' image of the wife, the hesitation before her reply, the phrasing of the question referring to a previous conversation, the confusion shown by the husband as the camera shifts away from him: all this suddenly addresses the viewer, telling us something about repression, censorship and the difficulty of filming social relations in operation, as it were. It also reveals that the conventional television-style image was based on the suppression of an essential bit of information: the man was to be filmed as if his discourse were 'open', spontaneous and autonomous, with nothing to hide.

In addition, the length of the sequence gives the viewer plenty of time to absorb the implications, on various levels, of the changes brought about by the pan. The film-maker's choices are made available for scrutiny, but more importantly, the interviewed individuals have ceased being simply individuals: they have been transformed into agents in and of a social situation. They have become representatives of a social order which includes and produces them. One could say that they have come to function as signifiers of a repressive order and an exploitative system hiding in plain sight. Conventional television techniques would have required the adherence to the obfuscations set in place by the interviewees, or would have lit the whole room and used fast stock to enable the handheld camera to roam throughout the room without hitting any unlit areas. Either option would have significantly impoverished the scene, aesthetically as well as intellectually, if those two aspects can be separated at all.

The camera movement marks a shift from the dialogue between film-maker and filmed people, which is the standard contract we see in operation in nearly all television, to a three-way relationship between the filmed, the filmers and the viewers, inserting that relationship in its turn into the whole problem of 'filming social relations'. In that sense, it is a critique of television documentaries and current affairs programmes, as well as of the propagandistic moralising characteristic of the populist videos which lack any sense of the dimensions of *mise en scène* essential to any notion of critical 'social' film-making. It may be worth mentioning that after this audacious shot, Gitai and his crew quickly went to the airport and left the country: during the interview, we learn that the man interviewed was an ex-cop and a former censor, while his wife described herself as involved in the security business. This sequence shot is an example of a courageous (left) intellectual at work with cinema. He does not tell us what to think but leaves us in no doubt as to what he thinks while providing a complex representation of a situation for us to argue with. The filmed people are not reduced to pawns in the film-maker's discourse of self-righteous indignation either: they are allowed to have their say and are shown as *metteurs en scène* themselves, that is, as people who not only engineer other people's lives, but who advocate an alternative kind of *mise en scène*.

The pan also stresses something few films and virtually no television programme ever acknowledges: the relation of otherness vis-à-vis the filmed which a film-maker experiences, but usually hides in the finished product. The images are not illustrations of a performed discourse on the topic, whether delivered on the soundtrack or not. Instead, Gitai shows us a way of making sense of an unfamiliar situation while participating in it, and he takes the viewer into his confidence, provided we are prepared to pay attention to the modes of enunciation and their implications. To arrange the same sequence into a series of separate, edited shots would have destroyed its productivity and made it into a sequence of bits dished out for us to follow obediently, linearly, ingesting whatever the film-maker wants us to swallow before getting a chance to reflect on the situation itself.

A little later in the same film, Gitai resorts to a different strategy but achieves a very similar effect. He shows a series of fairly brief shots depicting workers, in which each time the filmed people give only one single piece of information: their nationality. No other interaction between filmers and filmed appears possible and the otherness of the film-makers is writ large. As if exasperated by this inability to establish contact with the workers (the owner of the building contracting firm in Bahrain does freely interact with the film-maker), the sequence culminates in a shot in which the camera appears to be encased in a dark space, leaving only a small square of light with the heads of a few workers peering into the dark space below them, that is, towards the camera. One worker can be seen stretching his neck to get a better look at the camera, which seems torn out of any social context. It is removed from the scene, which is somewhere beyond the small square of daylight up above. Together with the viewer, who shares the camera's position and point of view in his or her own kind of dark, asocial space, gazing at a lit square high in front of his or her eyes, the camera becomes an object of curiosity rather than an investigator.

This sudden reversal of the camera's position and authority sets up a dialogue with the viewer, also barred from interaction with the filmed workers, but simultaneously enables the film-maker to engage in a dialogue with the workers, as if the removal of the film-makers and their camera from the social relations at work in the area were the price that had to be paid in order to enter into such a dialogue. After that shot, it is no longer necessary to specify at length in the film that the film-makers were allowed to work in Bahrain as long as they did not actively interact with the workers: that point has been made in the very *mise en scène* of the shot, signalling the gulf between 'us' (film-makers and viewers) and 'them' (the dislocated workers subjected to an extremely repressive situation).

In each of these two examples, the viewer's anticipated thoughts about the situation have been worked into its very mode of presentation. He is taking for granted our interest in critical, analytical looking and he assumes we will accord the images and sounds a degree of critical attention not normally given to television images, even though that is where the film will be seen by most people. He banks on a cinematic mode of attention in the sense that he relies on the fact that the forms of the discourse, such as small changes in the position of the camera, the pacing of the shots or their place in a particular sequence, will be noticed and thought significant. If we do not give these aspects of the discourse their full weight, the complexity of the social mechanisms filmed will escape us as well. We are not told what to think and neither are we asked to discover everything by ourselves (which always was a particularly cowardly and hypocritical aesthetic ideology anyway). Gitai films in a conversational mode, including his interlocutors in the process. Should a viewer refuse, or be too damaged intellectually to engage in this conversation, the films are transformed into somewhat slow, rather disorienting documentaries.

At the same time, this strategy has the merit of refusing to adopt a touristic point of view: the film-maker inviting the viewer to attend to his ruminations, illustrated by local colour shots linking bits of talking-head footage, as is customary in the vast majority of social concern videos, as well as in television journalism. Gitai thus shows up the insufficiencies, filmic as well as political and intellectual, that cripple both the dominant, touristic forms of documentary current affairs television and the unfortunately equally widely practised alternative form of journalism: the pretence of effacing the voice of the film-maker in favour of the 'authentic' voice of the people – an alternative that is at best hopelessly naive.

Finally, there is one more point I would like to make arising out of Gitai's film-making. Current debates in Euro-American film theory make a lot of play of point-of-view shots as ways of positioning the viewer in relation to the filmed. In many respects, discussions and analyses of point of view have taken the place of the former discussions about subjectivity and editing. Gitai's films, amongst others, show that it is most decidedly *not* through point-of-view shots that we are mobilized, but through the differences between, for instance, one point of view and another, even within the one shot. The dialogue with the viewer, which is the film's mode of address, is to be traced in the pattern of differences, in the shifts between markers, such as point of view manifested in the body of the text. That is where we learn who the film-maker thinks he or she is talking to, and what s/he thinks we know or are interested in.

Gitai's films assume an audience that is cine-literate in the best sense of the term: an audience that is interested in concentrating on the audiovisual discourse, on the way it is formulated, as much as it is interested in finding out how social relations have shaped whatever is being filmed. The films most definitely do not presuppose that we are concerned only with looking at the strangeness of others, nor is the viewer assumed to want to judge the people represented as goodies or as baddies. On the contrary, the films begin to make sense only when we regard the people represented as social creatures rather than as individuals in the conventional sense. We are not invited to give moral value judgments on the people, but rather to understand why and how they have come to be the way they are (by extension, the films ask us the same question). In other words, people are represented as shaped by social existence in all its contradictoriness with the consequent possibilities for change that such a view implies since the social itself is presented as a field in constant flux. Nothing is more alien to a Gitai film than the populist presentation of oppressed people as idealised victims. Even the historicity of film-making itself, the fact that different social formations circumscribe different practices and possibilities of filming, is part and parcel of Gitai's cinematic practice.

Although these techniques were developed in the context of a documentary practice, its lessons apply just as much to fiction cinema, where a subtle orchestration of time and space can be used to convey a sense of place, opening up the setting, the cityscapes and landscapes, to an awareness of historically accrued meanings. Gitai achieved this in his first feature film, *Esther* (1986), by setting a Biblical story in a recognisable and memory-laden part of contemporary Haifa, giving the viewers ample opportunity to savour the political sense generated by the mobilisation of this particular place for this particular story. In his next feature, *Berlin-Jerusalem* (1989), Gitai charts what happens to utopian desires while simultaneously affirming the need to have them. With impressive images (courtesy of Henri Alekan and Nurith Aviv), Gitai tells of the expressionist poet Else Laker-Schüler's yearning for an idealised Jerusalem, and of the Bolshevik

Mania Shochat, who went to Palestine and helped set up a rural co-operative, eventually becoming the main left opposition figure in Ben Gurion's Israel.

Instead of trying to re-stage the familiar Weimar iconography, Gitai uses a kind of cinematic shorthand, evoking the period through references, activating our memory banks full of representations of the period and the place. As he conjures up the Weimar setting in beautifully stylised sequences, Gitai simultaneously rearranges our perception of the Weimar period by putting into place three different but connected spaces. Our collective imaginary, made up of half-remembered films, photographs and paintings, provides the broadly historical setting. This imaginary space is then displaced and somehow hollowed out by the menacingly empty and shadowy spaces surrounding the poet in the first half of the film, while her private sense of claustrophobia and oppression is evident from the cramped and cluttered spaces of her private life. In two strongly emotional moments, Else escapes from these imbricated spaces: when she goes to the seaside and when she buries her son in a wintry graveyard, a moment marked by the complex tracking shot looking up through leafless trees at a pale sky.

The Mania plot-strand is also spatially circumscribed, from the trek across the foggy mountains to the place where the small group of pioneers set up their farming collective. From then on, the real but understated drama is in the way that the farm-space intersects with the Palestinian space around it. The film charts the gradually increasing sense of separation, together with the way such an isolated group living in back-breakingly difficult circumstances tries to weld itself together. Mania is the one with the most politically acute sense of the contradictions and dangers involved in such an attempt to act out utopian wishes: however much the members of the collective try to divest themselves from previous ways of living, people cannot but bring with them cultural and personal ways of being and thinking which undermine the utopian aspirations.

In the end, the political battle is over the way a particular state organisation seeks to enshrine and contain these tensions. The film ends more or less where the tragic dimension of the Israeli state begins, having shown that there were different options for that state. The relevance of the film to current political issues cannot be underestimated. It is the most explicit cinematic statement to date of a position which receives all too little exposure in either cinema or television: by showing the ideological as well as the experiential elements that were – and are – active in the formation of the Israeli state, Gitai points to the possibility and indeed the necessity of a *different* state formation, adjusted more realistically to the actual needs and conditions prevailing in the area. The film is neither pro-Israeli nor pro-Palestinian. In that respect, Gitai's film is a contribution to the growing debate about what it means to be an Israeli citizen and what the options in fact are.

Other films than Gitai's, made elsewhere (in Taiwan, India, Ireland), are also concerned with cinema's ability to render the complexities of time-space relations in such a way as to make us recognise spaces in which history can be seen at work, transforming spaces into places shaped by the encounter between social forces, personal experience and landscape. Gitai's films blur the distinction conventionally made between documentary and fiction: the sophisticated use of settings and location developed in his documentary practice is transferred into his features. At the same time as raising the question of the relation between the telling of particular stories and contemporary historical issues, this strategy brings that thorny problem into sharp focus by directly addressing the generation, and the historical-geographical reach, of a particular set of cultural forms such as, for instance, Biblical texts. In this way, the films also ask the question, rarely raised in cinema, of the social construction of audiences, while exploring the social construction of cultures. Hollywood and mainstream television solve those questions by reducing the cultural milieu to a picturesque backdrop for its dramas of individual character (and even those individuals are presented in exceedingly vague terms in order to make them internationally consumable). This reduces cultural meanings to those available to the average tourist. On the other hand, Euro-American experimental cinema contents itself with addressing specific subcultures while trading on generalities about art and aesthetic ideologies familiar throughout the West. Gitai, in common with a Kumar Shahani or a Ritwik Ghatak (at least in this respect), asks fundamental questions about the social aspects of cinema: at what point does a cinema betray its audiences by expecting them to become tourists in their own cultures? What is the effective geographical reach of the cultural material a film is fashioned from and which it addresses? How can one mobilise culturally specific meanings without at the same time restricting audiences to uneconomic levels, since such audiences will at best be numbered in the tens of thousands rather than in the millions required to amortise the investment costs of a major feature film? It is obvious from these questions that the answers imply political and ideological analyses rather than (or as well as) economic-industrial judgements. In effect, Gitai's films open up a whole new perspective on cinema itself: a new way of assessing how films are shaped by the tensions between their industrial and their cultural aspects.

I would like to close by stressing that in my view Gitai is a rare film-maker, one of an as yet small number whose work comes across both on television and in cinema by practising and requiring a fundamentally cinematic mode of attention to the audiovisual representation of social situations. In other words, he shows that television does not have to be as brutalisingly reductive as it is today. In addition, his approach to essayistic film-making respects the otherness of specific socio-cultural formations, but he does not allow himself to be traumatised by that otherness. His kind of conversational film-making offers one way out of the dilemma of being a local-specific intellectual locked into his or her own culture while being sufficiently outside of that culture to recognise its limiting boundaries.

ESSAYS

GITAI: THE NOMADIC IMAGE

Alberto Farassino

Translated by Judith Landry

Paradoxically, for a long time the cinema – born and named as a registering of movement – was linked to an idea of immobility. The movement of images on a screen was philologically, and thus 'scientifically' defined as illusory, a succession of fixed instants or photograms which only the odd and abstruse perceptual effect could reveal as self-propelled. But, above all, immobility was regarded as the chief characteristic of the conditions of the viewer: seated in a dark auditorium in a situation comparable to that of sleeping or dreaming, the spectator was seen essentially as a fixed entity, bemusedly admiring (non-existent) movement: a still point for the mindless absorption of images.

It is only recently that theory (such as Deleuze's writing) has once more affirmed the mobile nature of the image, indeed the positive identity between image and movement. Yet in its alternating shifting of focus between movement and fixity, or between screen and spectator, or between image-text and its perception, only rarely has theory actually concentrated upon where these images are born, or sought insight or confirmation in that original interchange between reality and celluloid from which every film is born. In any case, any theory of the purely apparent movement of the image would only have found confirmation, or a mirror of itself, in another realm of appearances: for a long time the studio, in Italian aptly named the 'teatro di posa' (literally: the place where one poses), was taken to be the actual 'place' where the cinematographic image was created, where every movement, every journey, every displacement could be recreated, compressed and summarised, with the final triumph of what we might call the paradox of the back projection/process screen where it was felt to be preferable to make the world move rather than the character, or rather the actor, or rather the star, a 'fixed' star if ever there was one. The prime purpose of much of the apparatus of the studio system (stand-ins, second units and so on) was precisely to avoid displacing those who had the singular privilege of remaining exactly where they were.

The freeing of the modern cinema from studios, as well as its occasional return to them – but intentionally, consciously, no longer merely for pressing technical or economic reasons – undoubtedly reflects a strong tendency towards reaffirmation, at a variety of levels, of the mobile nature of the cinema and of its creative process. But if modernity is rediscovering the linguistic-economic value of movement, it is postmodernity which is transforming movement into pure, non-teleological displacement, into vagabondage, wandering, nomadism. The journey, the flight, the search – once articulate and goal oriented – is being replaced by an absence of goals, of stages, of maps. The emigrant to the end of whose journey some destination, dream or myth could still be assigned, is now transformed into the landless, lawless nomad. U-topia is no longer the goal, unattainable but always conceivable: it is the permanent condition of existence.

Though wholly conceived and developed within the framework of the modern, the evolution of the cinematographic work of Amos Gitai seems to epitomise and summarise this transformation of the cinema from its classical to its postmodern phase. His filmography, viewed as one single film, tells of a passing from the certainties of construction, from the mutual solidity-solidarity between reality and image, to the demand for novelty offered by the movement of search and discovery, and then to the total dispersal and symbolic 'contamination' of the age of 'cultural nomadism'.

His first films, which are still those of an architect trying to 'make cinema', and who probably still believes in the documentary contract of the cinematographic shot, have as their recurrent subject what might seem to be the very reification of the ideal of stability: buildings, cities, fortified boundaries. But even *House* (1980), though entirely devoted to a house which becomes the set and studio for all the stories, already foreshadows the future mobility and mutability of his cinema. Wandered through by families, cultures and politics, the house/character of that film already strikes us as an open, fluid construction in perpetual transformation, apparently rooted to the ground but lacking any rock upon which to stand. And the almost contemporaneous series of films set in the Wadis around Haifa – valleys which become villages, river beds which become houses and fields – tells of a way of living and dwelling in which long familiarity with a place represents not so much the conquest of stability, but rather a permanent impermanence, an extended period of standstill in the wandering lives of immigrants, settlers, refugees. Gitai's investigations of the early eighties, as he travels between the United States and the Philippines, Bangkok and Bahrain, make up another phase of his journey. They are both the search for new professional horizons, new physical and cultural landscapes, and for identities which only total inattention to ethnic and religious matters could regard as unchanged over the centuries. Being Jewish elsewhere is being Jewish differently, and perhaps only the condition of the exploited remains the same under every sky and for both sexes.

But after *Field Diary*, which shows how the occupation of territory is identical with the occupation and repression of images (the only escape is through continual displacement, the elusive mobility of a film crew which works like a guerrilla commando), the progression continues from a documentarism which can by now no longer believe in its objectivity, to a cinema of fiction which seeks out more complex and tortuous confrontations, though no less risky and searching. Stylistically, it is also a progression towards a search for images and sets which might straddle time and space. It is the discovery of procedures like the sequence shot or long travelling shots which seem consubstantial with his extension of exploration to all fields of the cinematographic terrain (the discovery of actors, technicians, colleagues, directors, an attempt to co-opt cultural stars and cinephiles to his projects) and with the wanderings of his characters, which are both modern and eternal: Biblical figures or those of the Jewish cultural tradition now more clearly imbued with myth and at the same time wrenched from it by virtue of an attitude that cannot but be contemporary, and political. Thus *Esther* is both the kingdom of Ahasuerus rediscovered in the 'wadi' near Haifa, it is Persian miniatures seen in relation to the rituals and the ruins of the present-day state of Israel, it is the 'magical' and mythical lights of Henry Alekan restoring their historical depths to walls eroded by sun and time, it is the Straubian rigour and anachronisms, all of which now gain him entry into the most respected realm of the *cinéma d'auteur*. But it is above all in *Berlin-Jerusalem* that the history of a finished movement, the new search for the promised land by the twentieth century socialist-zionist movement, becomes bewilderment, disappointment, vagabondage. The aimless wanderings of Else through a land no longer recognised, through a city at war, amidst smoke and ruins, is the end of Utopia, where past becomes present and the absence of a place becomes the absence of or indifference to time. But the film also tells of the passing from a studio-based cinema, from the copying of style and manner, from a rigid chiaroscuro to a cinema of the land, of landscape, the desert, the aleatory nature of the shifting light of the Mediterranean.

And lastly, we have the Golem: the transformation of a myth of strength and stability, of the automaton conceived as an instrument of defence, an anthropomorphic fortress, the creature made of clay as a house is made of brick, into a nomadic figure, a mutant (in the very metamorphosis of the film's production plans itself: first some shots with Annie Lennox, then the definitive version with Hanna Schygulla) which confuses its own identity with that of the thousands of stories, old and new, in which it figures and with that of the places where it appears. The Paris of the emigrants, exiles and intellectuals replaces the Prague ghetto, the old industrial architecture is dematerialized, the very frontiers between bodies fall away. The Golem is the defender not of those who are confined within the ghetto but of those who have taken to the road. The images it arouses are not those of the certainty of the old stories but of those who have become nomads even in language and who derive sustenance from the 'contamination' of cultures, signs and styles.

ESSAYS

THE ROAD TO JERUSALEM

Mikhail Iampolski

Jerusalem plays a very specific role in Amos Gitai's work. As a geographical place, it is present only in *Berlin-Jerusalem* but it is there all the time as an invisible sign, organising the very structure of the films. Jerusalem is the symbol of the millennial dream of the Jewish people. It is not something that can be reduced to its concrete urban actuality. It is the end point of a road, the place of a mythical return, the promised land. It is the symbolic end of a journey, of a movement. Concreteness has nothing to do with it because it is at the same time a city from the Old Testament and the site of contemporary political conflict. It exists on many different levels, structuring to a large extent, as an all encompassing 'point' lacking any sense of concreteness, Jewish consciousness. It is no accident that for a long time the Christian tradition has distinguished two Jerusalems: the terrestrial one and the celestial city. A city which is both singular and double, which exists and yet is not.

In *Berlin-Jerusalem*, that city organises the narrative: that is where the film's two heroines want to go, where they meet each other and where the narrative ends. In this film, Jerusalem appears in all its chimerical aspects. It is a mythical city, Else Lasker-Schüler's poetic city, but also the city of the first Jewish migrants, an Arab city and a contemporary megalopolis. Its appearance at the end and its mirage, which appears from the beginning, bind the entire narrative into parallel layers tending towards a moment of fusion, a moment of genesis, towards the En Soph of the Kabbalah.

Jerusalem is not present in *Golem: The Spirit of Exile*, but in this film there is the sense of a journey, of a movement towards a mystical site. There is a slow, metaphorical movement along the underground canal towards the light shining in the distance and there is the same stratification of the city, stratified into something concrete, and a symbol. That the film was shot in France, partly in Paris, doesn't matter: again we have a film about a return, a movement, a pilgrimage organised around an invisible and unimaginable end point.

The plot of *Esther* takes place in Ancient Persia. As the film-maker acknowledges, the poetics of the film were basically defined by the creation of a synthetic image of the Orient in antiquity. But it was shot in the ruins of a deserted quarter of Wadi Salib in Haifa. The ruins, which represent the palace, create a strange kind of temporal tourniquet in the film. The action happens now, here, but the site of the action no longer exists and is represented only by traces it left behind. The space seems to bifurcate from the narrative and to escape into another temporal dimension, a kind of doubling underlined by the soundtrack which registers the sound of cars, airplanes, etc. within a Biblical narrative framework. It is as if the site where the action takes place didn't exist. The movement towards that site begins only towards the end when the actors, tracked by the camera, walk up a seemingly endless road, talking about themselves, removing the masks from their characters and re-covering their own faces.

The actor advances towards his or her own identity. A slow movement takes us from one era into another and the stratification gradually begins to cohere into unity. That kind of movement underpins all of Gitai's films and can be defined, for me, by the symbol of Jerusalem: a desired end of the road, a point to which no place can be assigned.

* * * *

This mythical point cannot be reached by way of a simple, linear movement. Granted, it is located at the end of a road but you can't ever reach it because it is imaginary. Long sequence shots and complicated travelling shots play a major role in Gitai's films but they generally appear in moments when space has become totally deformed, when you think you may have groped your way towards an exit leading to a place where people can't set foot. These sequence shots are particularly active in the 'Suburbs' of an invisible Jerusalem.

You may approach that point only by way of some magical procedures, which I will call 'ritual'.

The very appearance of the ruins in *Esther* stops the development of linear time. It was also in the 30s that Walter Benjamin, in *The Origin of German Tragic Drama* (1928; London: Verso 1977) and Siegfried Kracauer in his essay *Die Photographie* (1927) rightly connected the image of ruins to the interruption of time, to its utter undoing, disjunction, isolation. You can't escape from ruins. There is no direct way out of them (remember the image of the circular ruins in Borges). Even their basic formal appearance exposes the way dividing walls transform the site into a labyrinth, at the same time recovering the compositional structure of the Persian miniatures with their multitude of distinct zones held together by their ornamental character.

Esther is Gitai's most ritual film. Certain aspects of its poetics are close to the films of Sergei Paradzhanov and Jean-Marie Straub, surprising as the proximity to two such very different masters may seem. All of them have a habit of interrupting the flow of time with songs, dance, with complex gestures of deference and ritual courtesy. The entire plot of the *Bible* is based on the violation of ritual taboos:

Aman punishes Mordechai because he didn't bow before him, Esther risks her life directly addressing the King because ritual forbids a wife to present herself at the monarch's court without having been summoned.

Structurally, ritual is the magical evocation of a past event, the return of time, a cyclical movement of the subject. That is why it becomes the essential form through which a metaphoric Jerusalem is to be reached. The narrative structure of Gitai's films appears to be very contradictory. On the one hand, time hardly seems to move forward at all; the films seem to mark time in the zones of ritual, of song, of deferential gestures and awkward passages, in the areas where Biblical texts are declaimed. In between those fairly long scenes when the plot seems to have come to a halt, there are moments of narrative tension, with a very powerful drive which brusquely moves the plot forward.

Esther spends a long time walking to go and see the King, she spends a long time bowing before him, etc. Then, just one word from the King and Amman has already been punished; then another ritual pause and Mordechai is already Prime Minister. The action seems to be marking time but then it suddenly jumps forward. You get two opposite impressions: sometimes it seems as if Gitai is dwelling too much on detail and is too slow; at other times, he seems to be going too fast. The usual, conventional rhythm of narration is constantly broken. That feeling derives from the forms of magical movement: first, it circles around things and then it suddenly leaps into another set of conventions. That narrative structure is very closely related to that of Biblical narration, to the type of narration which is supposed to lead us to Jerusalem.

Gitai is a politically engaged director and his films are no strangers to didactics (in the Brechtian sense). Ritual, by the very repetitiveness of its actions, can be regarded as a technique of persuasion, of explanation and of analytical separation at the same time, as can be seen in Brecht. But the static character of the ritual scenes generates different ways of attending to them. Those scenes allow us to concentrate fully on the events themselves; they divert us from contemplation, which is fundamentally antididactic. Numerous scenes in Gitai's films exist in the interval of that contradiction between didactics and contemplation. The ruins of Haifa in *Esther,* the disused factory where the action starts in *Berlin-Jerusalem*, the near ruins in *Golem: The Spirit of Exile*, play an important role in his system of ritual and contemplation. The German art historian, Heide Schlüpmann, discussing the Kracauer essay on photography, wrote:

> Reproducing neither the inner connections nor the outward temporal flow of history, photography portrays only that which history is constantly evading and continuously passes over: the remnants of nature in it. The objectivity of photography is not nature in a positive sense, i.e. the immediacy of physis, but rather nature as the negativity of history. When photography records history it simultaneously annihilates every historical context. *(New German Critique,* no. 40, Winter 1987, p.103).

A ruin is a historical sign that has escaped from history. It is history constantly overcome by nature and only as such does it become an object of contemplation because history itself cannot be contemplated. The whole of history resides in its linear, progressive character. It is all theatre and text, punctuated by lessons, by didactics. Alekan's cinematography in Gitai's films, the ruins functioning as decor, losing any relation to history, to linear temporality: all that contradicts the didactic pathos of the films even though the director justifies it by referring to Brecht's distanciation praxis.

History is destroyed by ritual itself, which contradicts the very notion of a linear development and traditional causality. Nevertheless, ritual transforms history into a text. Because of ritual repetition, the action in many scenes begins to break into clearly subdivided blocks, forming something like chapters, sections, fragments and even distinct gestures. When creating *Esther,* the director wanted to equalise the length of sequences by refusing montage within a given episode. When the personification of the narrator had to appear in the sequence, he emerged suddenly into the foreground from underneath the horizontal bottom line or the vertical edge of the screen, never integrated into the scene so that its body remains free from cuts.

Such a cinematic kind of subdivision corresponds to another subdivision that has fundamental importance for Gitai's work: linguistic gesture. Cinematic ritual is based on verbal ritual, on the systematic use of Biblical texts, ritual songs, poems (for example those of Else Lasker-Schüler in *Berlin-Jerusalem*). Linguistic gesture is often superimposed onto the film's hieratic scenes as in the funeral rite in *Golem: The Spirit of Exile.*

Linguistic gesture imparts a cadence to the action, punctuating it, giving it a quasi-poetic structure. In *Esther* and in *Golem: The Spirit of Exile*, Gitai uses the same extended quote from *Ecclesiastes* that speaks of the enduring things on earth, of the vanity of history:

> For everything there is an appointed season, and there is a proper time for every project under the heaven; a time to be born and a time to die; a time to plant and a time to root up what is planted; a time to kill, and a time to heal; a time to wreck and a time to build; a time to weep and a time to laugh; a time to mourn and a time to dance; a time to cast away stones and a time to gather stones; a time to embrace and a time to refrain from embracing.

The essential point is one of subdivision, dislocating the flow of time and separating out distinct units. In *Golem: The Spirit of Exile* a creature emerges, resembling the golem which is constructed by means of a cabbalistic combination of letters. The entire Cabbalah is replete with that combinatory, subdividing spirit Gitai reconstitutes in his films. The denoted reality of the universe seems enchanted by the word threaded through it. In *Berlin-Jerusalem* German expressionism clearly left its mark, an influence motivated by the story as well as by the period. More unexpectedly, that influence can be felt in *The Spirit of Exile*, where Hanna Schygulla's make-up recalls Wegener's *Golem,* while some sequences bring *Metropolis* to mind (the spirit's appearance in the Eiffel Tower sequence). The cinema which achieved the maximum fusion between the literary and the plastic arts, the pictorial, is that of German expressionism. It is the cinema of a poetic rhetoric and pathos.

So, the road to Jerusalem capriciously winds its way, at times even tracing Dante's circles, with metaphoric twists and turns evoking the journey of Bunyan's *Pilgrim's Progress*. He crosses spaces torn out of history, accompanied by incantations. In other words, that history follows the path of the ruins barely accessible to reality. In *Esther,* the beggar-narrator enounces his monologue and returns to his profession, asking for alms but doing so in a place where there are only a few children and almost nobody else. His pleas address emptiness. Elsewhere in the film, a royal proclamation is read out in a bizarre courtyard with just a few chickens and dogs. The word addressed to the world remains in its cage, within its ruin, its pigeonhole. Gitai's films are built in such a way that their basic structure, their formal framework is ceaselessly put under pressure from within by some natural force alien to it. In *Esther,* for instance, that natural force can be identified as the flaming tongues often present within the frame. In *Berlin-Jerusalem* the literary ritual of the heroine is destroyed by the appearance of another fire: the pyres where the Nazis burn books (a particularly significant scene if you think of the role played by citations from books in Gitai's work). In the whole trilogy, ritual is presented as a particular form of violence to which another even more terrible kind of violence is opposed: murder, death, war, terror. Ritual can lead to death, as in *Esther,* but death itself surpasses the limits of ritual and destroys the structures it preserves.

Reality erupts into the film as something sudden and lethal, like the gunshots, the explosions, the chaos in *Berlin-Jerusalem*. This incursion by 'reality' into the film is constructed like a kind of ecstatic opening towards the limits of the text . Reality erupts like something ecstatic and subjects the universe to a transfiguration. A conventional world of ruins is transformed into a convulsive world of violence at the end of *Berlin-Jerusalem*.

Ecstasy is a passing beyond, a rupture in the structure of the text, a rupture in the cyclical movement, the opening out onto a straight road. Ritual repetition brings closer to us a Jerusalem that exists outside of history. Ecstasy allows us to reach it, as at the end of *Berlin-Jerusalem*, to reach it as a reality and not just as a symbol. All Gitai's fiction films end with a long travelling along a straight line, like a ritual movement crowning and celebrating the escape from (the ritual of) shooting.

Berlin-Jerusalem

AN ARCHITECTONICS OF RESPONSIBILITY

Irma Klein

'For a tear is an intellectual thing'
And we are always sifting through our lives.
Darkened, with no other choice,
Words spring out of the stone,
Slow forming as the stone,
The heart's matter in a different form.

Nathan Zach, *Wessex* [1970; transl. Gabriel Levin].

About a year ago, *Zmanim [Times]*[1], an Israeli historical quarterly published a double issue devoted to the relations between film and history. The volume included the proceedings of a conference of Israeli scholars at the Tel Aviv University, as well as additional material by other scholars. Although such an event may seem routine, this is not so in Israel where the number of books published in Hebrew which can be described as 'film theory' is negligible even though universities have run film courses for over two decades.

However, after an extremely eventful quarter of a century of Israeli history (twenty five years of colonial occupation of the West Bank and Gaza, fifteen years of Likud government), the bulk of the issue is devoted to the holocaust and the second World War era. The historical moment from which *Zmanim* attempts to speak is not itself historicized. History, for *Zmanim*, seems to be 'over there', while cinema is 'over here'. The historian's role would then simply be to bridge the two.

One contributor, Anton Kaes, does manage to articulate part of the problems which cinema poses to history when he describes the images registered on celluloid as a 'technological bank' which forms and socialises the collective memory. He emphasises the danger of blurring the distinctions between collective and personal memory, the risk of detaching memory from its grounding in time and place, the fear that film is perceived as an eternal present, that is to say, as an eternal return of history as film. According to Kaes: 'History today is totally "democratised" and socialised through the technical media of photography, film and television; all foreignness has been driven out of it. Television in particular has trivialised history into easily accessible information bites or shallow entertainment; history no longer engenders experience.'[2] Quite rightly, Kaes joins those who realise with anxiety that the media, cinema and television, have become the central instruments for the formation of historical consciousness. What seems to be at stake today is precisely how that historical consciousness defines both the horizon of expectation and the limits of disappointment for the historian.

Most of the Israeli contributions to *Zmanim* pass in silence over the potential and the problems of documentary cinema. Yossi Mali, for instance, only sees the mode in which documentary film provides evidence for general historical research, cinema being 'totally trivial' and unable to 'raise any problem of special interest' for the historian. What interests him is the 'historical fiction film' because 'this is what evokes a true interest in the spectator, which is the real problem for the historian'. This leads him to identify 'the truly profound problems' as the questions relating to the compatibility between cinematic experience and historical consciousness as such. Mali's conclusion, invoking the pioneer of historiography, Huizinga, is that 'any reader of history would admit that one well staged scene has more validity than all of Huizinga's words'.[3] The historian's lack of attention to the historicity of his own discourse results in the promotion of a politics of illusionism: it is through illusionism that the spectator will come to historical knowledge. For Mali, as for many others in Israel, films, or indeed cinema as a whole, seem not to have a history and remain outside of the historian's domain. Cinema, having no history, no historiography, it follows that there is no need for a theory of the historicity of cinematic discourse itself. Within the historian's discourse, cinema vanishes as a historically specific and significant medium and is subsumed within the generic category and content of mass media.

Among the many things missing from *Zmanim*'s discourse are the core questions posed by the journal's ostensible topic: why cinema and history in the first place, and what makes the juxtaposition of these two terms different from, for instance, pairs such as history and literature, history and philosophy, art, and so on? What is the particular specificity through which we might start defining the problems of cinema in the face of history? The singularity of the question, its difference and separation from all the others is to be located in a specific historical moment: that of the emergence of the photographic image in the historical arena. Its problematic epistemological status, its ontologically inscribed plenitude, its excess of meaning resisting signification: all these are implicated in the most fundamental problematics of Western culture. Both theoreticians and film-makers have conceptualised and developed their aesthetics according to the way they have confronted these issues.

The nature of the moving photographic image, its activation of duration, is one of the central factors which drastically altered our perception and conceptualisation of history. Indeed, in a move described by Kracauer as 'the all-out gamble of history', it transformed our very experience, in history, as historical subjects. The abundance of screen memories inscribed on celluloid has permeated our consciousness to a degree where differentiations between personal, collective and popular memory risk losing their edges leaving little room for grounding historical experience in specific times and places. The extensive 1970s debates around notions of popular memory and narrative addressed these very questions. In historiographic as well as in film theory debates a critique of narrative forms was elaborated focussing on the way representational practices masked and naturalised their operations, inducing a sense of perceptual mastery of both the past and the present. Via the mobilisation of Emile Benveniste's linguistic distinction between the levels of *'histoire'* and *'discours'*, between the levels of the enouned and the enunciation, Christian Metz's film theory problematised the suppression of the marks of enunciation in cinematic narrative, endowing it with a semblance of transparency. Narrative cinema, according to Metz, presents itself as 'a story from nowhere, that nobody tells, but which, nevertheless, somebody receives.'[4]

The need to historicize discourses by historicizing the positions of addresser and addressee has become a major commitment shared by film theory, historiography and by certain film-makers. The spread of notions of postmodernity has made the historicising project even more urgent. A different understanding of historicity has evolved out of the encounter between historiography, linguistics and psychoanalysis. This new historicism takes into account the discursive aspects of experience. Hayden White has suggested that history is to be viewed as a narrated sequence; Fredric Jameson proposed the existence of a narrative political unconscious and Michel Foucault considered history as a succession of dominant discursive protocols, cultural epistemes separated by discontinuities. For Foucault, the historical document does not grant access to history. On the contrary, history is one way in which a society recognises and develops a mass of documentation with which it is inextricably linked. Whereas traditional forms of history undertook to transform the monuments of the past into documents, in our time, Foucault claims, history transforms documents into monuments.[5] For him, the document is implicated in the discursive operation of power, that is to say, the regulation of the production of knowledge. His work must be confronted if we are to understand the function of the cinematic document as well as the cinematic institution in the domain of historical enquiry and knowledge production. Such a critique of historical consciousness also implies a reconsideration of modernisation and, by extension, of the nexus between modernism and the camera's intervention into history. This in turn refers us to the famous thirties debates addressing the relations between aesthetics and modernism associated with the names of Lukacs, Bloch, Benjamin, Brecht, Adorno et al. This intellectual constellation remains a crucial reference point for any contemporary consideration of the connections between film, history and consciousness, not only in Israel.

* * * *

Amos Gitai, of course, is not mentioned in *Zmanim*. His absence from this volume only prolongs his virtual absence from two other recent historical accounts of Israeli cinema[6]. This systematic extraterritorialisation of Gitai is truly remarkable: it is a significant absence of a man whose work consistently and lucidly addresses the very questions evoked by historians. The whole of Gitai's work is informed, indeed shaped by the search for a film-making practice that will produce both cinema and historical consciousness at one and the same time, the one indistinguishable from the other. In this respect, Gitai's work addresses precisely the horizon of expectations of the anxious historians while returning historicity to the practice of making sense with films.

The artist Tamar Getter writes: 'Because of the special historical and cultural circumstances of Israel, there are no usable cultural images "from outside" in the European or the American sense: we have no Christian narrative (nor our own tradition of painting), neither a bourgeois nor a clearly capitalist narrative. What we have is the Zionist narrative, but almost all its images exist in verbal language and they do not hold any clear visual presence or formulation. [T]hey do not present [a]ny particular optical traits of the type one could be confronted with when looking at Marilyn Monroe or a crucifixion. [T]hat which was already a "ready-made" cultural image on the linguistic level was merely a formless subject for a painter. [O]ne would have to invent images as a pictorial possibility.'[7]

Like Gitai, Getter belongs to a generation of artists born and matured in Israel who entered the field of art in the early seventies when there was a widespread preoccupation with the impact of photography on the forms and the contents of Israeli painting and figurative representations in general.

Although her remarks address the issues she seeks to confront in her own practice as a painter, her pictorial problematic engages with the issue of 'location' and has other interesting affinities with Gitai's cinema. Like Gitai, her concerns are also tied to a complex historical discourse about the 'character' of an Israeli culture facing the Scylla and Charybdis of particularism and universalism as they have, by now, come to be projected onto notions of the relations between East and West. In Israel, this dialectical trajectory of the continuing debate concerning the character of Israeli culture[8] goes back to the generation of the thirties and the forties when poets like Shlonsky and Altermann saw their practice as embedded in the construction of a collective identity for a young, aspirant 'national' culture. This constellation is especially significant for an understanding of the radical shift in the sixties with the emergence of the personal, private self in Nathan Zach's emphatically enounced 'I', signalling the arrival of *'discours'* in the nation's cultural *'histoire'*.

'One moment silence, please. I beg you. I want to say something' says Nathan Zach in 1960 amidst the noisy phraseology and pathos of collective Bengurionism as he articulates the breakthrough of the private self in the Israeli poetry of that decade. With this line[9], according to the literary critic Nissim Calderon, Zach signalled the writer's distance from the political public sphere. In his attentive critique of Zach, Calderon noted that this distanciation became 'the ID card of the writer' since history had become suspect and the political sphere had turned dangerous. History and the political had become non-literary, even anti-literary elements and Zach's 'I' constituted an injunction to a whole generation of Israelis to read and write ahistorically. Calderon continued his analysis by pointing to the appearance in poetry and prose of abstract individuals outside of any kind of *histoire* altogether, 'anonymous persons, Israelis whose being Israelis was of no importance, into whose lives nothing Jewish permeated, [a]n abstraction of time, space and place, [a]n algebra of human situations. [E]ven in a poem in which there is a port and a mountain, Zach remained strictly abstract in not mentioning the name of Haifa, a city in which he spent some significant years of his youth.'[10] Calderon relates the shift marked by Zach's 'I' to political dilemmas and a sense of intellectual suffocation in the fifties which contributed to writers' sense of revulsion from notions such as 'Jewish Morality' and 'The Tradition of Israel', as if there were only one such morality and one such historical tradition binding together all Jews. Rather than to face up to the ever increasing complexities of the historical situation, Calderon suggests, history itself came under suspicion. The need to reintegrate biography and history remained as if blocked, an impossible desire still to be fulfilled.

1973, the year of the Yom Kippur war, marks the return of history in the form of a renewed and detailed attention to the physiognomy of the landscape and of its inhabitants. That is when David Perlov started shooting what was to develop into an outstanding six-hour *Diary* and when Amos Gitai, who belonged to a different generation, followed suit making his first 8mm films. Perlov called for a politicised Israeli film culture, proposing a cinema in which biography and geography would constantly intersect and interact, cutting the personal and the collective, the private and the public into a single flow. The landscape returns as a major pictorial reference in Gitai's work, where it functions often as a site condensing collective memory traces. Indeed, it is difficult to read Gitai's films without acknowledging the importance of this sense of 'knowing the land'[11]. However, Gitai does not present the physiognomy of the land as an equivalent for the landscape of the soul or states of mind. Rather, Gitai strips the ironic masque off 'Yedi'at Ha'aretz', rendering the landscape as surface through the camera's 'objectif'. In this respect, he extends his fellow architect Kracauer's suggestion that the photographic reproduction of nature 'has to allow the psychic permeation of those images to take place not in order to imbue nature with a soul but, on the contrary, to produce the photographic view of soulless reality [s]een from the "eye which anticipates love"'.[12] In his turn, Gitai does not wish to fill in, to bridge or suture the ruptures in time or in representation, the gaps between past and present inherent in historical time. This is in fact what Gitai's films systematically avoid. Instead, the films are designed as invitations for us to think and rethink discontinuities, requiring the viewers to try and understand history as marked by the deepest fissures. For it is precisely the failure to perceive history as continuity which opens up the space for the emergence of historical consciousness and defines the way history may be traced in cinematic representations. Consequently, Gitai orchestrates a cinema that uncouples narrative from history, transforming story into discourse while chronicling the collisions between personal, collective and popular memory, awakening the spectator to the process of remembering and the complex processes that anchor one's body in a specific spatio-temporal history.

* * * *

BAIT. The Hebrew word means both 'home' and 'house'. The Hebrew language does not differentiate between the two and thus effaces the boundary between inside and outside. The distinction between the space enclosed by walls and its surroundings, earth, soil, landscape, whether urban or rural, is lacking. And since the Hebrew language does not differentiate between the two, the difference is also missing from Jewish and Israeli consciousness. For Israelis, Bait stands for Home (the land, the state of Israel, the space, the building). It is just as metaphysical as it is concrete.

The Bait is the place where we live and its connotations form an integral part of Jewish-Israeli collective memory. The return to the Bait has been the central Jewish aspiration for millennia, since the fall of the first temple, the first Bait. The trauma caused by the destruction of this piece of architecture has forged an enduring correlation between notions of independence, sovereignty and a stone structure, opposing the Bait to the concept of 'Galut', exile.

In *Zakhor*[13], a particularly interesting book on historiography and collective memory in the history of Israel (meaning here the history of the Jewish people), the author, Yerushalmi, argues that Jewish society lost its historical consciousness in the period of exile going from the fall of the temple to the 19th century. The society's self image had become static and contemporary events no longer seemed significant since it was the *Bible* which constituted the referential model against which all current events were tested. Each pogrom, every disaster was projected onto the 'original', archetypal catastrophe, thus falling into the mythical groove of an immobilised collective memory.

Zionism, among many other things, set itself the task of pulling the Jewish people out of this vicious circle of exile. As a product of the 19th century, Zionism adopted that century's notion of modern nationhood, staking a claim to the possession of both land and a language, the two most salient features of a nationalist ideology. Zionism understood national sovereignty to be the fundamental precondition for a historical culture and set out to constitute the 'modern Jew' by making him/her a sovereign being. As a movement for national-Jewish liberation and sovereignty and a revolution in consciousness, Zionism undertook to make the new Jewish subject the master of his own house/home. The crucial and unprecedented aspect of this revolution was a linguistic one: Hebrew, a dead liturgical language, was turned into a living mother tongue for all those who, in exile, had come to inhabit dozens of different languages.

In the Balfour Declaration of November 2nd 1917, His Majesty's Government said that it 'viewed with favour the establishment in Palestine of a national home for the Jewish people.' This too is an additional notion of a Bait. And after the holocaust, that Bait has become an urgent shelter into which all the hopes and aspirations together with all the contradictions of the Jewish and the Zionist histories have been channelled.

Zionism's dream of a Bait is tied to two other houses as well. One is described by Gaston Bachelard in *The Poetics of Space*[14], the other is that of cinema. Both are linked to the historical moment in between the onset of industrialisation and the upsurge of urbanisation, when the experience of time is being systematically transformed into spatial categories. For Bachelard, the house is one of the greatest powers of integration for thoughts, memories and dreams of mankind whose binding principle is day-dreaming. It is body and soul. Under the pressure of urbanisation, the space of Bachelard's house could not endure for the urban masses and around the turn of the century it collapsed in favour of the construction of another, very different form of space which in many ways addresses the unconscious of Bachelard's house: the cinema house devoted to day-dreaming and other manifestations of desire and regression.

Bait / House

In fact, one could locate the entire panoply of problems of Zionist-Israeli identities and their historical-ideological perspectives in the tensions between notions of Bait, of house/home and its extension into the concept of homeland. Bait then offers a configuration of the Zionist ethos, the locus of its embodiment, its public as well as its private spheres. And this is precisely what Amos Gitai addresses when he confronts 'the house' in his documentary film known simply as *House* (1980). The house in the film functions as an indexical imprint of an historical process, a space condensing antagonisms and tensions. Intuitively allegorical, Gitai's camera moves towards that complex series of topographical, historical, ideological, economic and political contradictions encapsulated in the space occupied by that house. The house is a ruin. It has no walls. It is merely a frame, a spine, showing traces of its former oriental ornamentations. The movement of the camera and of people going in and out of the house turn its spaces 'inside out' like the surfaces of a Moebius strip. The house is being renovated. It is a piece of real estate functioning as a metaphor for the present Israeli state apparatus. The house has a new owner: an Israeli professor of economics. He bought it from an Algerian-Jewish couple who lived there since the mid-fifties when it was confiscated by the newly born Israeli state which regarded it as an absentee-property when its Palestinian owners ran for their lives during the 1948 Israeli War of Independence.

The story of the house coincides with its history, in relation to its ownership as well as its authorship. The film questions and problematizes both. The house as product, as discursive space, is scrutinised through the investigation of the division of labour and the procedures governing its production. Through Gitai's particular selection of scenes, through his aesthetic preferences and interviews, we become aware of the geopolitical and socio-economic complexities of both past and present times. Through the personal and biographical stories, evoking histories, narrated by each speaker in turn, the spectators' attention is drawn to their own blind spots, to that which they are unable to see, identify or tell, that is to say, to the place and function they unknowingly have in the historical process.

The conceptions of Zionist ideology are reviewed: instead of being the condition of human social relations, Zionism is revealed to be the ever so human practice of the social. And Gitai gives the house its historical volume by taking his camera on a long, abrupt movement cutting through the space of the house to the refugee camps on the West Bank, today the home of the Palestinians working on the house. The house is an oxymoron, simultaneously everyone's and no-man's land. We cannot know the house from its inhabitants. Our spectatorial positions are in constant movement, shifting from one point-of-view to another, displacing perspectives, destabilizing any secure position we might think we have in the face of history. Soon we realise that while we are witnessing the rebuilding of a Bait, we are in fact experiencing its falling apart, its collapse into perpetual disintegration. What was *heimlich* has turned *unheimlich* as opposites coincide. The movement of the film is that of consciousness and its temporality in the domain of the uncanny.

What is being dismantled and shattered is our imagined position as coherent, unitary historical subjects. We are the ones whose historical being is being disrupted and put up for grabs. Hence *Bait* marks, in Israeli media history, the site of a suppression: Israeli Television censored its transmission and tried to deny it an audience. The film seems to activate the past Jewish and currently Israeli fear of 'graven images', now mummified in film, epitomised in the Hebrew anagram Re'iya-Yier'a (sight/fear/awe). conjuring up a terrifying excess of cognition, what Lacan referred to as the knowledge that 'cannot tolerate one's knowing that one knows.'[15] The censorship of *Bait* enables us to glimpse an overlooked continuity in the interstices of apparent discontinuity, as if recalling the words of Walter Benjamin: 'Allegories are, in the realm of thoughts, what ruins are in the realm of things.'[16]

* * * *

ESTHER. Set and shot in the contemporary area of Haifa known as Wadi Salib, *Esther* (1986) conjugates various memory layers, different historical times, monuments and narrative styles. Even though their conjunction does form a coherent unity, the differences between the elements must constantly be kept in mind. Unlike Jerusalem, Haifa is neither a sacred city nor a city nourished by conflict. Unlike Tel Aviv, Haifa does not signify the Zionist Renaissance. On the whole, Haifa seems like a rather nice city, calmly nestling on the periphery of politics and concentrating on its commercial development as Israel's industrial port. In the past, however, it was the centre of the Arab intelligentsia and the heartland of Arab politics in Israel. At the time of the British Mandate, it was administered jointly by three mayors: one Brit, one Arab and one Jew. For some years it was called Red Haifa. That was where the workers' syndicate, Histadrut, was founded in 1922. It was also in Haifa that the decision was taken to make Hebrew the national language.

In the very heart of Haifa, Wadi Salib was an Arab quarter until the war of 1948. In the fifties, it was turned into a refuge for the masses of Jewish immigrants coming from Morocco. In 1959, Haifa saw the political uprising which marked the first major outburst of antagonism between European and Oriental Jews (Ashkenazim and Sepharadim). Haifa's municipal government decided to disperse Wadi Salib's population and destroyed the quarter. *Meoraot Wadi Salib*, the Events or the Riots of Wadi Salib, was the title of a sixty minute film Gitai made for Israeli Television in 1979. Many of he Arabs who had been born in Wadi Salib and fled their homes in 1948 later returned to find their homes destroyed. Besides, an administrative decree forbade them to live there. So the Arabs went to live in another quarter, Wadi Rushmia, where some Eastern European Jews, survivors from the concentration camps, had also settled. Gitai made a film there too, first in 1978, then again in 1980 and in 1991. All these histories and films are part of the texture of *Esther*. There is also the reference to as well as the images and the sounds of the moment when the film is being made, Haifa 1985.

And then there is the Biblical text with its own narrative and historical temporalities. In the *Meguilat Esther*, a scroll addressing historical consciousness, the *Bible* presents history as a process of repetition, an apocalyptic promise to be fulfilled in time. In proposing that the compulsion to repeat forms one's destiny, the Book of Books locates Truth on the side of historical stasis while overtly presenting the narration of history as the victor's narrative, legitimising his account of the events leading up to his ultimate triumph. However, in the Israeli collective and popular memories, the point of the Biblical story has been forgotten. None of the students or the friends I tested could remember, in spite of their efforts to do so, either the beginning or the end of the story. Nobody was able to remember that by the end, the victims had turned into oppressors. Neither were they able to recall the story started with a woman, a Queen called Vashti, who refused the King's order to come and display herself. She refused to be reduced to her, in Laura Mulvey's phrase, 'to-be-looked-at-ness'. The King's advisers, terrified by the prospect of women rebelling against patriarchy, suggest that she be replaced. Esther is the replacement. A remarkably interesting beginning for what will end up as a catastrophe. Even more so when it appears to have been erased from memory. On the other hand, the repressed has a habit of returning, imbuing reality with the dimension of allegory: Purim (in Hebrew, 'pur' means destiny) is the only festival devoted to destiny, repeating itself every year as a unique, secular holiday and carnival. Whatever else Purim may be celebrating overtly and consciously, the erasure of the story's precipitating event, the woman's refusal of her destiny as an object for the gaze, persists in the festival as a corrosively allegorical subtext, present in the form of a blind spot.

Esther

In Gitai's *Esther,* the screen is turned into a palimpsest of spaces, places, landscapes, all manner of memories (personal, collective, popular, not forgetting the director's own stock of screen memories) and temporalities. The narrative constellations figured on the screen become the locus, the projection space of spectatorial experience. The film's 'action' is no longer locked into the confines of the frame but constituted in the encounter between viewer and film, with intertextuality opening out that space, energised by the dynamics of consciousness itself, towards a historicizing practice.

The Landscape in *Esther* is that of the Wadi Salib ruins. Again, Gitai places his actors in an oxymoronic space. While enacting a historical spectacle, a 'costume picture', they are deployed according to the aesthetics of Persian miniatures. The *mise en scène* does not show but creates the aura of a palace while the disposition of the actors recalls *tableaux vivants* embedded in sequence shots which intensify the suggestion of a continuum in historical as well as in cinematic temporality. For Guy Debord, the dialectic of closeness and distance at work in the spectacle turns into an opposition, the social separations alluded to being concealed under the cloak of imaginary unities. Gitai's critique of the spectacle is of quite a different order. He collides the spectacular against the miniature, the ruins of Wadi Salib against the suggestion of a palace, sustaining a double dialectic of closeness and distance, leaving the differences in plain sight while inviting the viewer to gear his or her reading to the emerging tensions and dehiscences. In other words, the sense of unity and continuity prevailing in the film nevertheless leaves the ruptures unconcealed, because it is through these gaps that the viewer's historical subjectivity enters into the picture. It is precisely the refusal of the chimera of historical reconstruction, acknowledged as impossible, which enables the historicization of the spectator to become part of the cinematic texture.

Through the acoustic presence of sirens, cars, airplanes and the like, as well as through the occasional camera pan away from the Biblical diegesis, the Haifa of 1985 abruptly emerges into the Biblical time. Through the judicious orchestration of image and soundtrack, Gitai offers a sublation of both Bazin's commitment to the integrity of spatio-temporal blocks and Eisenstein's assault on the photographic image's ontological realism. Gitai's montage often articulates spaces to each other, not in terms of temporal juxtapositions but in depth within the same shot, arranging further collisions between spaces as well as temporal layers. However, Gitai's film refuses to engage in the conflict between classical modernism and realism. His film does not seek to create the illusion of an imaginary spatio-temporal unity, but neither does the film run aground on the fetishisation of 'discontinuity' and ruptures. The joins, the 'edits' within the shot as well as between shots, between the image track and the sound track proliferate and come to constitute a discourse in their own right. The most cogent account of the productivity of Gitai's conjoining Wadi Salib and *Meguilat Esther* is still Walter Benjamin's text on dialectical images:

> It isn't that the past casts its light on the present or the present on the past. Rather, an image is that in which the past and the present moment flash into a constellation. In other words, an image is the dialectic at a standstill. For while the relation of the present to the past is a purely temporal, continuous one, that of the past to the present moment is dialectical: not of a temporal but of an imagistic nature. Only dialectical images are genuinely historical, that is to say, not archaic images. The image that is read, I mean the image at the moment of recognition, bears to the highest degree the stamp of the critical, dangerous impulse that lies at the source of all reading.[17]

The 'location' has been transformed so that its elements can connect with and critically dislocate the historical constructs operating in the mind of the spectator, inviting the formation of more complex and differently articulated types of historical understanding. The experience of film viewing, or rather, of viewing this film, thus urges us to experience our own bodies as 'in history' and awake to consciousness.

Finally, there are the actors. They too form an additional intertext. Their very presence engenders, for those who know what other roles they have played in Israeli cinema, a series of revealing cross references. Moreover, as their narrated autobiographies, at the end of the film, collide with the roles they play in the *Meguilat Esther*, the weft of histories that constitute the text becomes denser still. The 'Biblical' characters, already encrusted with meanings derived from their presence in popular and collective memories, are allowed to reverberate not only with other fictional characters incarnated by these actorial bodies in Israeli cinema, but also with the narrated personal biographies of the actors. Rather than allowing the actors' personal present and past histories to be insinuated into their fictional-historical characters, the film does the opposite: it insinuates echoes of the Biblical story into the lives of the actors and, by extension, into the body of Israeli cinema as a whole. In a dialectical subversion of the politics of identification, we are enabled to awaken to the histories, both past and present, which constitute and sustain 'us' in an intimate distance from the histories we imagined to be ours. With a shock of recognition, the ending turns into a beginning as Gitai cuts, with a leisurely but relentless travelling shot (repeated at the end of many of his films), the textures of the present into the very fabric of historical experience.[*]

Notes

[*] I would like to thank Tamar Getter for her help and encouragement.

1. *Zmanim*, edited by Idith Zertal, no. 39-40, Winter 1991.
All translations from Hebrew are by the author unless specified otherwise.
2. Anton Kaes, *From Hitler to Heimat* (Cambridge: Harvard University Press, 1989), p. 126.
3. Yossi Mali, 'Is History Photogenic? Historical Film in the Post-Modern Age' in *Zmanim*, pp. 74 sqq.
4. Christian Metz, *Psychoanalysis and Cinema – The Imaginary Signifier* (London: Macmillan, 1982), p. 97.
5. Michel Foucault, *The Archaeology of Knowledge* (London: Tavistock, 1972), p. 7.
6. In Ella Shohat's *Israeli Cinema – East West and the Politics of Representation* (Austin: University of Texas, 1987), Gitai's 'significant films' are mentioned without further comment. In Igal Bursztyn's *Faces as Battlefield* (Hakibbutz Hameuchad 1990, esp. pp. 184-5) only two of Gitai's films are mentioned, *Wadi Rushmia* (1978) and *Bait* (1980). In the half-page devoted to the former film, Bursztyn wrongly claims that Gitai set out to poeticise poverty and 'primitivism'.

7. Tamar Getter, 'Thoughts on Paintings 1976-1989' in *Kav Art Journal*, no. 10, July 1990, p. 43.
8. This trajectory cannot be understood adequately without fully taking into account the complex impact of, for instance, 'Knaanism' and 'Ofakim Hadashim' in Israel's art practices and in Israeli culture in general.
9. In *Shirim Shonim* [*One Moment*], 1960.
10. Nissim Calderon, *A Previous Chapter – On Nathan Zach in the Early Sixties*, Hakibbutz Hameuchad 1985, p. 10. Three years after *Shirim Shonim*, taken aback by the extent of his stance's success, Zach published an autocritical essay entitled *Worldless Literature* (in *Yochnai* no. 4, eds. Nathan Zach and Ori Bernstein), arguing that by 'worldless', he meant a reference to a shared, specific landscape and social reality. Calderon's analysis of the forces in play and indeed Zach's own account of events as well as the way he addressed the issues at stake in his poetry are far more complex than my quotes suggest. However, a more detailed analysis of this extremely challenging debate would take us too far into the broad field of Israeli cultural studies and will have to await another occasion.
11. The importance of the connections between landscape and collective memory is illustrated, for instance, in the rituals of A'avat Ha'aretz, loving the land, and Yedi'at Ha'aretz, knowing the land. The latter was even a compulsory course in elementary school inculcating, through a 'knowledge' of sites and names recognised from Biblical times, a sense of historical continuity in Israelis' collective memory. The construction of such a sense of continuity was fundamental to the incorporation of a sense of 'Moledet', homeland.
12. Heide Schlüpmann, 'The Subject of Survival: On Kracauer's Theory of Film' in *New German Critique* no. 54, Fall 1991, p. 120.
13. Y. H. Yerushalmi, *Zakhor*, Seattle 1982.
14. Boston: Beacon Press, 1964 [*La Poétique de l'espace*, Paris 1957].
15. Jacques Lacan, Seminar of 19 February 1974, unpublished but quoted in Shoshana Felman, *Jacques Lacan and the Adventure of Insight*, (Boston: Harvard University Press, 1987).
16. Walter Benjamin, *The Origin of German Tragic Drama*, Transl. by John Osborne (London: New Left Books, 1977), p. 178.
17. Walter Benjamin, 'Theoretics of Knowledge; Theory of Progress', transl. Leigh p. 39.

A VIEW FROM WITHIN

Taline Voskeritchian

To its many supporters, one of Israel's great strengths has been its ability to steer a political course based on humanistic ideas and nationalistic contingencies. Within the perennial tensions created by these twin forces, Israel has managed to project the image of a haven under constant threat and, by implication, in need of perpetual protection from real and potential adversaries.

Yet the growth of the state of Israel from a seemingly modest homeland for the dispossessed to a regional superpower has generated a tradition of often anguished debate about the viability and consequences of pursuing a policy of peace and security, based on the oppression of another people. In recent years these peripheral protests have become increasingly vocal, and voices from 'the other Israel' have questioned the uneasy alliance between humanistic ideals and tough militarism. Though less known than some of the other participants in this debate, the Israeli film-maker Amos Gitai has confronted the dilemmas facing Israel in two recent films, *House* (1979) and *Field Diary* (1983). Ironically, neither film has been seen by the audiences for whom it was intended. *House,* a fifty minute documentary, was initially produced for Israeli television and, despite its ambiguous, bittersweet tone, never shown in Israel; *Field Diary* was filmed entirely in the occupied West Bank and South Lebanon, and completed in France where Gitai presently resides. Between them these two works present a vision of Israeli society which is, at once, eloquent and tragic, angry and hopeful. But equally significantly, the differences between the two works bear witness to the changes which have taken place in Israel over the past five years and to the ways in which these changes have left their mark on the consciousness of those outside the consensus calling for peace.

The ostensible subject of *House,* declares a narrator at the outset of the film, is the renovation of an old Jerusalem house which once belonged to the Dajani family, and the film is to record the progress of the project. But as the structure begins to impose itself on the benign skies of the holy city, a rival structure of human relationships and attitudes begins to emerge, and the film gradually shifts its attention from the architectural enterprise to the lives of the people who are linked to the house. Gitai listens to them all intently, recording their words and gestures, and occasional silences, prodding gently here and there or allowing the awkward moment to spend itself out. The new owner of the house, an enterprising Israeli academic, talks enthusiastically about the plans for the second and third floors. The aging, personable Jewish couple from Algeria describe with amusement the financial transactions which led to their eviction and relocation. Toward the end of the film we meet the original owner of the house, a wise, somewhat melancholic physician, who remembers his childhood in the house with his seven brothers, his quick escape during the 1947 war, and his subsequent return after the 1967 war. His account of the meeting with the new owner is particularly moving—a mixture of distress and affection—as he recounts the polite yet awkward exchange between the two men. The Israeli contractor supervising the renovation and his son talk with pride about the 'perfect economic alliance' which they have established with the Palestinian masons who are brought in each day to do the actual building. It is these workers, often silent and sometimes articulate, who receive Gitai's most sympathetic and sustained attention. They talk resolutely about their work and about the need to stay put for as long as possible. Like the original owner of the house they see the passage of time in large strokes, with patience and irony. Several times in the course of the film Gitai returns to them, not only to talk, but to capture their sheer being as they pound the

Bait / House

large limestone slabs with an obsessive thud which remains in the viewers' mind long after the film is over. It is their constant yet insidious presence which Gitai tries to capture, to underscore the fact that the alliance between the Palestinian worker and the Israeli contractors is not only imperfect but downright brutal.

Yet despite the emphasis which Gitai places on the exploitative relationship between the dispossessed and the occupiers, *House* does not see Israel as a polarized society. On the contrary, from amidst the differences between the Palestinians and the Israelis, it tries to articulate similarities. At the conclusion of the film the Palestinian worker kneels in supplication to thank his god and express his undying devotion. This image of prayer becomes the ultimate rite within which conflict and suffering are neutralized. The only recourse for the Palestinian worker is religious faith which nourishes his soul and, more importantly, makes the task of living under occupation a little bit more tolerable. Likewise, the Israeli contractor and his son seem caught in an equally powerful web of forces. More than being about the renovation of a house for an Israeli family, *House* turns out to be a document about the very people whose displacement has made this architectural project possible. For the Israeli contractor, his faith in the pioneer spirit of the early settlers is the only way out of the terrible burdens which the presence of the Palestinians places on him. Both the contractor and the masons inhabit a stifling landscape where faith in a transcendental truth coexists with the knowledge that the individual in Israel – Zionist and non-Zionist alike – constantly sees his reflection in his adversary. In this respect the film in its intent is potentially subversive, claiming one thing and being another, and in so being offers itself as another parable for what Israeli officialdom says and the reality of the situation: that the Palestinians are not only present but they are inextricably intertwined into the everyday life of the Jewish state — economically, psychologically and morally.

Unlike *House*, *Field Diary* is a longer but more urgent, nervous film, conscious and indignant of the changes in Israeli life and anxious to provide a corrective to the prevailing truths. The pathos of *House* is replaced here with a harsh, stark picture of an increasingly militarised life. While *House* is content to let its 'heroes' speak, *Field Diary* attempts to forge a moral and political mission for its documentary intent, a mission which goes beyond the confessional mode and takes clear positions on matters of peace and war.

Field Diary opens in front of the residence of (the mayor of Nablus) Bassam Shaka'a as his wife engages in an extended conversation about the occupation and its concrete results for the people of Nablus. This conversation is periodically interrupted by the Israeli soldiers whose hands cover the screen and whose threats of confiscation are heard in the background. These early interruptions in the flow of the film have a sobering effect on the viewer, for they underscore both the fragility of the activity of film-making and the resilience of the final product. The progress of the film is continuously accompanied by its antithesis—by the threat of its destruction. These twin qualities motivate *Field Diary* to develop both as a chronicle of life in the occupied territories and as a tribute to the insurrectional aspects of the medium. The dual posture is maintained throughout the film as Gitai reminds his audience of the self-consciousness with which he is approaching his subject, and the imperatives which he and his crew face as they travel throughout the occupied territories in search of the opposition viewpoint.

The film is a series of entries in the diary of the film-crew, and each entry cuts the flow of the film with bold chapter insertions about the contradiction between what is projected to the world and what actually takes place in the occupied territories. Far from being just a self-expressive exercise the 'writing' of the diary becomes a dangerous activity, a struggle between those who maintain the consensus and those who film its contradictions and inner fissures.

Within the tense context of occupation, the film exposes rather than hides its sympathies and allegiances, continuously reminding the viewer that the activity of making such a film in Israel requires dedication to peace and justice. In the struggle to tear open the rigid facade of the prevailing consensus, Gitai spends some time with a group of Israeli settlers joyously exploring the rugged landscape; he details the brutal arrest and manacling of a suspected Palestinian troublemaker, he focuses on a bored yet discreet exchange between two Israeli soldiers who discuss the best way to solve the country's obsession, and, most poignantly, he rummages through the human debris of a devastated Palestinian refugee camp in Lebanon. Taken together, these entries into Gitai's public diary catalogue with an inner violence of their own the pressure points along which Israeli society plods: the settlers, the military machine as it operates internally and as it executes expansionist adventures into neighbouring territories, and, of course, the victims of the military machine and the enthused settlers, the Palestinians themselves. Gitai's visual presentation of the victimized Palestinians is memorable as he moves slowly through the human suffering of the camp, focusing on a woman's weathered face, an old man's limp walk, a child's puzzled gaze into the distance. Yet, amidst the outrage, Gitai seems to find some sobering and hopeful signs within the very elements which constitute the polarized state of Israeli soldiers. In the former he sees the energy of youth tempered and disciplined by suffering and oppression. The camera engages in a facetious race with him as he runs in and out of crowds and rubble, while the film tries, perhaps unsuccessfully, to catch up with him. In the latter he sees the possibility of change and re-definition of national priorities. From time to time the film returns to the two soldiers as if to record the unfolding of their argument. As the film moves to its conclusion, their viewpoints diverge: statehood or total annihilation. Then the discussion is totally polarized, the soldiers become aware of the camera's intrusions and the film ends on an affirmative note, as they hurriedly move away from the unflinching determination of the camera, receding quietly into the background. For the film-crew and, vicariously, the audience, the struggle against the threats of confiscation and destruction of the medium deliver certain victories. With the image of the soldiers disappearing into oblivion the film comes full circle, affirming its mission; as the harbinger of truth and the vehicle for re-definition and, hopefully, change. If not checked the war machine will eventually turn in on itself, transforming the ideas of peace and security into mechanisms of entrapment and hopelessness. Despite continuities between *House* and *Field Diary*, the differences between the two works —differences in style and tone — highlight the changes taking place in Israeli society and the

Field Diary

effect of these changes on the everyday life of the population. Gitai cautions against the systematic militarization of Israeli consciousness, and the gradual polarization of Israeli society. He argues that behind the elaborate structure of the state — efficient and awesome as it is — is the ugly underside of the state. Despite the political posturing and militaristic adventurism of recent years, Palestinians will not go away and cannot be wiped out; they are there in the occupied territories and their very presence needs to be confronted, accepted and acted upon.

Gitai's critique of the alternative to peace raises, once more, some of the fundamental questions around which much of the debate from the 'other Israel' has centred: can Israeli society be both humane and militarized, given its Palestinian underside? Is it possible to have security and peace when a considerable portion of Israel's population feel alienated from the social, economic and political fabric of life? And, what will be the long-term effects of an increasingly militarized policy on those in whose name the rapid militarization takes place? Gitai proposes these questions to the viewer simply and unassumingly, focusing his attention on the wear and tear of everyday life in Israel—its tenuous joys, its harsh conditions, its pervasive pathos, and its complex identity. *House* and *Field Diary* are painful reminders that the fate of the Israelis is firmly and inseparably intertwined with that of the Palestinians. The recent twists and turns have in no way tempered this ironic, violent interdependence. On the contrary they have confirmed what Gitai and others engaged in the debate have held all along: the Palestinians and Israelis are historically bonded to each other and real, lasting peace will benefit not only the Palestinians, but it will also heal the Israeli contractors and soldiers.

(Orig. publ.: *Journal of Palestine Studies,* no. 50 1984)

ESSAYS

BROKEN DREAMS – THREE GITAI FILMS
Pineapple, Esther and *Berlin-Jerusalem*

Ashish Rajadhyaksha

Since *Esther,* Amos Gitai's cinematic restlessness seems to have found some concrete direction.

His work has always moved, it appears, in massive circular formations. The restlessness of his recent film, especially, seems to lead him into some kind of an inexorable cycle of time-determination that would recoup for itself those smaller, more fragmented moments that usually seem to present us with our subjective choice. He has worked at a particular edge of historical time, an edge that always was uncomfortable with the promises of change and which, now that history has revealed itself in all its bad faith, cannot afford to be isolated any longer from its own impulses.

Hannah Arendt, whose remarkable writings on the meaning of revolution have given such strength to dispossessed peoples everywhere – whose writings, indeed, I am inevitably reminded of whenever I see Gitai's work – has something to say that could be of value here:

> Antiquity was well acquainted with political change and the violence that went with change, but neither of them appeared to it to bring about something altogether new. Changes did not interrupt the course of what the modern age has called history, which, far from starting with a new beginning, was seen as falling back into a different stage of its cycle, prescribing a course which was preordained by the very nature of human affairs and which therefore itself was unchangeable. (*On Revolution*, New York: Viking Press, 1963)

Gitai's cinema, in the way he makes it, the violence he personally undergoes and contains within himself, in order to present his view of change to us, posits more than anything else, a crisis of sheer living. It is a crisis that any individual working in dis-location with his own (subjective, personal) history would, I think, recognise: of having to fall back, even, I would say, regress, into certain nostalgic formulations of history at a time when the very effort to formulate a course of historical action can prove annihilating. For Gitai's entire practice, in a sense, contradicts the idea of history as 'pre-ordained by the very nature of human affairs', but to achieve it he also has to isolate himself from his audience, isolate himself – even render himself – by his courage. Like his actors in *Esther,* who have lived in reality the history that they have now to play-act in order to present it to us; like Gitai himself, a shadowy reflection in the windows of the shops and bars of Jerusalem at the end of *Berlin-Jerusalem,* the practice has had to remove itself a step so that it can pitch its own vitality against the regressive circularities of history, in order to be able to say that, even though as an example of human existence this film may be just one of many, it is imperative that it be enlivened at least by the particularity of what it shows and says, here and now.

More than any other film-maker I know, Gitai has pitched himself, his courage, against this wall: he is, indeed, renowned for his ability to dare, and it comes across as a crucial aspect of his earlier work. (Yussef Shahine: 'Gitai is such a courageous person that I would be surprised if he weren't admired throughout the Arab world. I have seen his films against Begin at a time when the latter was very, very powerful. Gitai dared. He dares to go very, very far. For me it is the duty of a cineaste to dare. If you don't, what is it you want your films to say?'). To dare, you have to have faith in the future, as you leave behind all your moorings in identity and risk your very self in a sort of historical wager. Many people do dare, precisely because they believe that, as Shahine has put it, you have to dare if you want to say something. But until now, I have never been so struck by the extent to which the very notion of daring can be culturally determined in the forms it takes, in the battles it articulates.

To dare is to take a step forward when there is no going back:

His Rhodus, hic salta!
Here is Rhodes, here: leap!

Gitai actually makes this leap in a film like *Pineapple;* he points to a Rhodes, a giant conglomerate spreading its tentacles from Hawaii to the Philippines, an enemy completely present even as it draws back, returns with new strength and recoils before the prodigiousness of his aims, a world he can isolate in a death grip so as to actually show what is beyond. Here he can slice through the circularity of time, draw from the awesome, the grotesque tandav that girdles the globe three times over as it produces its commodity, to actually breathe a living pulse on his soundtrack. He can do it because he dares, but also because it's there.

How different the scenario looks when Mania Vilbushevitch-Shochat (Russian revolutionary, active in the intellectual circles of Berlin, a founding member of the Kibbutz and the Israeli labour movements), a woman fresh from an assassination attempt on the Tsar – from an era almost over-determined by the convergences that made it up, moment to moment – walks through the desert with her comrades and looks at her land as if to say, 'This too must have a history.'

The difference is, of course, that here regression can take place; indeed, the greater part of the film shows just how certain norms of what those in power would call the nature of human affairs can take the very idea of change back into a more primitive –

primitive in every sense – notion of history. Gitai enters into this space; he does it most self-consciously, following the whirl of a Berlin basement with all its Wagnerian charms and slogan-shouting (as a red flag engulfs the camera, at one point), with a series of slow right-to-left camera tracks as Shochat and the men move into another space, one whose movements have an inexorable, even fatalist, flow. Looking at the people trying to reap that land, I thought of the Indian anthropologist D.D. Kosambi and his description of the role of the monsoon in this subcontinent:

> The urgent need for a working almanac lay at the root of astronomy, algebra, the theory of numbers, all of which were conspicuously Indian (specifically Brahmin) achievements. The season could then be foretold even when the sun and the moon obliterated their starry background. Primitive reasoning led inevitably to the conclusion that the heavenly bodies not merely predict but form the all-important weather. (*An Introduction To The Study of Indian History*, D. D. Kosambi, Popular Prakashan, Bombay, 1975, p. 250)

So these men and women walking into this land, introducing history, accelerating the dynamics of change, could be its new Brahmins too. The point is that whatever be the course of change, it has to be lived through, its great cycles of domination experienced before the world beyond is glimpsed. With *Pineapple* Gitai could perform that leap, experience and suffer the stultifying definitions of change as proposed by an American multinational, and encapsulate a global system in a camera-tilt showing a Filipino peasant's hands in the soil. In *Berlin-Jerusalem* he must take his people with him, suffer not on their behalf but with them.

In one of the definitive theoretical interpretations of Gitai's kind of cinema, Paul Willemen has spoken of a film-making that would explore 'the interconnections between story and history, representation and subjectivity, its emphasis on a critical analysis of a historical process that includes, and thus historicises, questions of subjectivity and narration', working with a means of discursive layering that would permit a dialectical, 'complex seeing'. It seems to me that a film like *Berlin-Jerusalem* needs this kind of multiple historical/discursive layering as much to, so to speak, distribute the burden. *Esther,* the film that launched him on to new explorations that have led now to *Berlin-Jerusalem*, seems in this light the more successful though less ambitious film; there, in working the inverse currents of an extreme-fiction moving gradually against a strong ideological undertow to extreme-documentary, Gitai was able to work in the multiplicity of his own authorial voice. Here, integrating the violence of his own courage into the landscape Gitai moves to the edges of time and of action, launching those investigations that would yield the history that Mania Shochat and Else Lasker-Schüler sought from their own opposing poles. In Amos Gitai's own words:

> These people have a sensation that they can and will build Utopia, and that by going to another place you can do it. Of course, the biggest crisis that Jews face with Israel is that it is not a Utopia. That's why it is difficult for them to take criticism in Israel. The dream is broken. I think most civilisations have these concepts that they will be able to construct a Utopia. It's just that they are left with a broken dream.

PART II
The FILMS

1 BAIT

Serge Daney   Julian Petley   Mikael Harsgor   Stuart Klawans

Serge Daney: When the film begins, to the deafening sound of a bulldozer, the house changes ownership – it is being rebuilt. The house doesn't stop changing. It was there before Israel existed. It was a lovely Palestinian residence. Then it came to be part of those 'unclaimed' belongings routinely allocated to Israelis. Moroccan Jews lived in it for a long time. Today it is a university professor who will move in. Gitai wants this house to be both a symbol and something very concrete; he wants it to become a character in a film. He achieves one of the most beautiful things a camera can register 'live', as it were; people who look at the same thing but see different things – and who are moved by that vision. In this crumbling shell of a house, real hallucinations begin to take shape. The film's central idea is straightforward and the film has simply the force of that idea, no more, no less. The camera fuses with the idea (but doesn't serve it, thank God). In order to speak of that house and that land, Gitai recovered that exceptional emotional quality. *House* was made in 1980 for Israeli Television. Annoyed, they censured the film. Tel Aviv lost its cool faced with a dryly serene film. (*Libération*, 1 March, 1982.)

Julian Petley: Like *Field Diary*, *House* is distinguished by Gitai's willingness to let people speak for themselves in long, uninterrupted takes, or simply to watch them at work. In the final scene, for instance, when we return to the quarry, the camera simply observes, from above, three Palestinians at their daily routine. By conventional standards, the length of these two, largely static shots is excessive. In context, however, like the images of the house itself, they take on all sorts of meanings and associations, evoking a concept of time very different to the Western one, a concept in which the present occupation and its attendant miseries are rendered transient indeed. (*Monthly Film Bulletin*, June 1985.)

Mikael Harsgor: Opinions are heard which might not be pleasing to a nationalistic ear; and this is probably why the screening of *House* was banned: because the masters of the Israeli TV are afraid of Israeli material of Gitai's kind.

They prefer ordinary Israeli viewers to be entertained by *Love Boat* or to follow, with bated breath, the life of the Ewing family living in a majestic mansion outside Dallas. For Israeli TV, Texas becomes the Holy Land, our new spiritual centre – synthesis of Echad-Ha'am [Zionist philosopher] and JR. (*Ha'aretz*, 22 June, 1982.)

Stuart Klawans: When some Israeli newspapers claimed he had made *House* for the Palestine Liberation Organisation, Gitai replied, 'I offered it to Arafat, but he doesn't buy films in black and white.' (*The Nation*, 5 June, 1989.)

2 *WADI*

Angelika Kettelhack   Susan Barrowclough

Angelika Kettelhack: Wadi Rushmia is located in the east of Haifa, a valley between the Carmel Hills and the Haifa Bay. During the time of the British Mandate it was used as a quarry and was later abandoned. From 1948 onwards different groups began to settle in the Wadi: new Jewish immigrants from North Africa and Eastern Europe who came from the temporary immigration camps, and Arabs who were expelled from their homes. The Arabs were defined by the law as 'Absent Present', meaning that their right to use their property or to live in their homes is denied: 'absent' because they were absent from their homes at a specific date in 1948; 'present' because they exist physically in Israel. Because 'Absent Present' Arabs cannot use their property or live in the houses they used to own, some of them squatted in Wadi Rushmia and built themselves a shelter.

The people of the Wadi built their homes from city waste. Car tyres and barrels are used to cover roofs, to build a small bridge and to prevent the steep cliffs from eroding. Shutters, pieces of wood and parts of boxes are used for construction. In such a place and under such conditions people must co-operate in order to survive. Good relations developed among the people, Arabs and Jews. The common day-to-day problems created solidarity rather than hostility.

Iskander, an Arab fisherman, and Myriam, a Hungarian Jewess, live together by the cliff. Further down the slope live the Jewish brothers Iso and Salo. Yussuf and Aisha, an Arab couple, live a few houses away.

Iso and Salo have been plagued by suffering and tragedy. Throughout their lives they have been constantly uprooted and forced to wander looking for a safe place to live. Their defensiveness, their constant search for a place to rest after years of wandering, epitomizes some of the intentions of the Jews when they established their own state. Iso and Salo, in their shack, continue to be subjected to the iniquities and the lack of understanding of the outside world, and their sense of instability remains. They survive in an abstract world of unfulfilled expectations which makes their specific tenacity absurd.

Yussuf and Aisha, also living on the valley floor, were born in Wadi Salib in Haifa. Like other Palestinian Arabs, they were displaced by the 1948 war. Since then, they are considered 'Absent Present'. 'Somebody told me "You are just an Arab", so what if I am an Arab, did I come from abroad?' Yussuf asks.

Being in a Jewish state, Salo and Iso feel somehow superior to Yussuf and Aisha, yet they know that they have to co-operate with the Arab couple in order to survive. Yussuf and Aisha have their own way of dealing with Salo and Iso's latent attitude towards them. They know that on a hot day you sit and sip hot tea to dispel the heat, and they watch with the slight amusement and irony that comes from being a native and so close to the land while Salo and Iso suffer the heat of the sun. In this way, Iso and Salo are newcomers to a strange land and they are unable to accept or relate to its specific physical conditions.

On the other hand, Myriam becomes sensitive to the land; she has developed an understanding of her context. She has planted trees on the cliffs above to protect the houses below from the glare of the midday sun and to produce a slight breeze. (Young Film Forum, Berlin.)

Susan Barrowclough: Gitai takes small concrete situations to exemplify larger ideas. In *Wadi,* his subjects do not represent a microcosm of Israeli society, but the possibilities of that society. Living in the ruins of pre-1948 history, in a forgotten hole, they have found a way of living together. Yussuf is homeless in his own backyard but he has memories of an attachment to this land which official designations, like the absurd 'Absent Present' category, cannot wish away.

In giving the voiceless a voice, he has cut through the impersonal certainties of political rhetoric to admit the pathos and intensity of self-portraiture. As a subject, Wadi might even be seen as an optimistic counterpart to *House.* Yet, for a film whose intent is to show a small example of co-existence in a country at war with itself, Gitai has made a strange narrative choice. The three families are never shown talking together. Their physical proximity is evident and they constantly refer to each other. But, in their isolation from the mainstream of Israeli society, they also appear isolated from each other, overwhelmed by their plight. (*Monthly Film Bulletin*, June 1985.)

Wadi

3 FIELD DIARY

Selim Nassib Yann Lardeau Julian Petley

Selim Nassib: We are in the occupied West Bank (Jordan). The camera finds some Israeli soldiers and sticks to them relentlessly. Impossible to make it turn away – the shot lasts minutes and minutes, absolutely steady, beyond what is normally allowed in cinema. The soldier, or the farm-owner, or the young Israeli coloniser begins to feel more and more ill at ease, loses control, shouts, demands that this look be stopped, puts his hand over the lens – one of the victims of this insistent gaze attacks the camera-woman, knocks her over, hits her. But in spite of everything the camera keeps rolling with a breath-taking obstinacy, with a matter of factness which is the most remarkable trait of the Israeli national character. Amos Gitai is a young Israeli director. He films without complexes. But what bothers the involuntary heroes of his *Field Diary* so much? It is that the unbearable camera is like an inescapable mirror. Look. Look at yourselves. You are the occupier in action. You are a soldier of an army of occupation. The reflection quickly becomes intolerable. Except for those who have lost all sense of morality and blithely state that one must 'annihilate the Arabs', the people who exercise such a domination, such a merciless appropriation, prefer to do it out of sight of indiscreet eyes. The whole film is based on this process of a steady and unflinching glare.

Those who are occupied, the Palestinians, are also subjected somewhat to the same treatment. But for them it is different. They have the smiling tenderness of the vanquished who must bear it and wait. The camera remains equally fixed, but the people of the West Bank – the deposed mayor who lost his legs in an attempt on his life; the farmer who sees his fields melt away like snow in the sun of colonisation; the stone-throwing child – don't take this steady look as a form of aggression.

In the Judean desert, during a funeral ceremony with Israeli flags, we see Menachem Begin addressing the ancestral spirits, telling them the Jews 'have returned whence they sprang'. In a field, Palestinian women circle around, waving one arm, then the other (the Palestinians of Sabra and Chatila made exactly the same gesture the day after the massacres) in lament as their hundred-year-old olive trees are ripped out in order to make room for a new settlement. These two series of images are particularly striking because they exceed, wordlessly, the specifically political dimension of the conflict and illustrate the weight of culture, of history, of the dead in that corner of the planet condemned to be without peace. (*Libération*, 4 January, 1983.)

Yann Lardeau: An ethics of the travelling
The soldier asks for the sound-man's papers. Indeed, for him, the film crew is suspect. He forbids the filming. The exchange is brusque, sharp. We are in front of the mayor's wife as she enumerates the vexations caused by the military surveillance of their house. The officer has put his hand over the lens of the

Field Diary

camera, but it keeps filming the image of that obstruction, of this prohibition to see and to show, the enforced blindness of the military solution. That sane image returns often. True, the very presence of the camera provokes something. Israeli soldiers, Palestinian farmers, refugees and colonisers: what the security forces cannot control in front of the camera is its point of view, which thereby escapes their control. The soldier also knows that the camera targets him as would a rifle-sight and yet, in spite of that, it doesn't aim to aggress him. The insistence of that gaze weighs heavily, but the camera's movements are without violence and rather tender. There is a simple relationship between the area that governs the soldier's actions and the survival of the warrior: who is not with me is against me – that is precisely the fake opposition the camera refuses to engage with. It doesn't present itself as an enemy, and yet it doesn't look for alliances either: it is careful to remain outside of such a construction of the world, of such a factitious grid that orders the military destruction of a territory, of a society. As such the camera introduces an alien element into the conflict, an eternal presence, the aim and motivation of which becomes totally undecidable and therefore 'suspect', as the officer guarding the mayor's house says. It has become a third eye, that of conscience, an eye one knows never to be a good one. A *Field Diary* is a testimony, a description of things seen, informed by and reflected in a conscience. It is thus essentially subjective and doesn't pretend to be exhaustive on the subject ...

The film consists of about fifty sequence shots conceived as autonomous 'capsules', mostly shot from a moving car as if this were its inseparable carriage, the moving base of the camera. The road is thus transformed into an endless travelling, stretching across the occupied zones, with pauses, occasional stops, slowing down, with emphatic moments. Here, more than anywhere else, the travelling becomes a question of morality. At the beginning, in the identity check scene, we see the film-maker quite clearly, but the general rule is that we only hear him, from the other side of the image, from the side of its manufacture. From the combination of the voice-off with the travelling along the road, it follows that we never enter into the reality of the war, but that we always remain on the edge of the scene, at a tangent to it. The camera constantly slides over its subject without ever penetrating it, aggressing it, just as our eyes slide over the surface of the screen. In that way the camera reproduces within the film our real position as viewers. Gitai films precisely the borderline between the civil world and the military world, a borderline set by the civil world for the military institution. It would be wrong to expect some sort of confirmation of this film from Middle East specialists: it is the opposite pole of the theses propounded in editorial offices. Professionally, the media have opted for the military solution: they operate with a war scenario and do not imagine any other, always pitting Palestinians against Israelis. The media only talk of the balance of forces between adversaries, their firepower, the magnitude of the damage, the number of human lives lost, the capability to resist, the international repercussions. Amos Gitai, however, films the war in the Lebanon at its weakest point, three months before it exploded, when it wasn't yet a war, but when there was no longer any peace; when the annexation of the West Bank hadn't yet caused the departure of the Palestinian farmers, but before the colonisers have got fully installed; when the situation is still ambiguous, undecided, in between two destinies, as if caught in a hesitation... Gitai doesn't confront two nationalisms. He films behind the Israeli lines: the subject is considered an internal Israeli matter... From one shot to the other the opinions expressed do not make contact with each other, but they end up outlining the image of the country's human geography, a torn image, caught between two antagonistic poles but not reducible to the expression of that opposition. While it is always easy to denounce a war, even to the point of becoming captivated by its fascinating spectacle of horror and of conveying nothing but that fascination (*Circle of Deceit*, 1981), *Field Diary* offers a civilian image of war, making it a symmetrical counterpart to Ici et Ailleurs (1976) and setting it apart from the rest of audio-visual production by its content as much as by its mode of operation, by the solution it offers to a problem that pertains to the ethics of the film-maker as much as to the aesthetics of cinema. (*Cahiers du Cinéma*, no. 344, 1983.)

Julian Petley: As remarkable as Gitai's long sequence shots is the way in which they are edited together. Sometimes this works in an effectively simple, dialectical fashion, as when an interview with a settler who talks blandly of the beautiful view from his new home is followed by the scene of the olive trees being uprooted, or when a scene of a Palestinian family harvesting their wheat leads to another showing United Nations flour being handed out in a Palestinian refugee camp. Sometimes sound and image work in resonant counterpoint, as when a lengthy travelling shot from a car surveys land confiscated from the Palestinians, accompanied on the soundtrack by an Israeli radio play for children explaining the importance of national roots and attachment to the land. These two different forms of montage culminate in the film's most powerful sequence, which takes us from the commemoration in the Judaean desert of an Israeli hero of the first century AD to the invasion of the Lebanon and a visit to a pitiful refugee camp, linked by a Jewish funeral prayer on the soundtrack. It's a sequence of which Humphrey Jennings could have been proud, and which forcefully and imaginatively brings home the specific historical and political dimensions of the present conflict, uniting past and present in a richly associative pattern of sounds and images. (*Monthly Film Bulletin,* June 1985.)

Field Diary

4 ANANAS

David Lusted

A documentary tracing the international network of the Dole Pineapple Corporation through interviews, images and intertitles connecting the company's headquarters in San Francisco, its production bases in Hawaii and the Philippines, and a can-labelling factory in Japan.

It is a powerfully persuasive exposé of the extent and complexity of a typical American company's economic penetration, attendant labour exploitation and social oppression in representative Third World countries. And, in its formal construction, it is an arousing challenge to conventional documentary modes. Importantly, the success of the exposé is intimately connected to the challenge of its form.

From the first interview with a Dole Corporation agronomist, framed asymmetrically in an armchair, redundantly illustrating his poolside lecture with a still life painting of tropical fruit, to the concluding detail of labelling machinery receding into the middle distance of the frame, it is apparent that *Pineapple* is about much more than story-telling, observation or explanation. Its considerable power arises not through the prevailing forms of investigative journalism, ciné-vérite observation or even agitprop, but through challenging the claims for veracity, transparency and objectivity made for these modes of film-making by their supporters.

Pineapple eschews the ethnocentric voice-over narration and voyeuristic camera characteristic of ethnographic films, for instance, by giving its many interviewees the luxury of time to speak for themselves rather than, as is more customary, being spoken 'on behalf of'. But this is not in order to practise an alternative faith in the naive realism of their performances. Those of the Third World (like the cheerfully stoic 64-year-old emigré fieldworker in Hawaii or the wiseacre Philippino village-leader), if not comically set up the better to witness the foot-in-mouth act of those from the First World (like the doleful Dole descendant, the Director of Labor Relations and Head of Security – an apt twinning of responsibilities under the Philippines' Marcos régime – and the Company's intermediary priest and missionary), do not escape the camera's critical eye.

Director Amos Gitai's strategy is neither to ridicule nor to sanction his subjects. Rather, it is to undermine the security of the audience in the transparency of what is said and seen, to encourage scrutiny of what they represent rather than judgment about the kinds of people they are. The effect is to read, as it were, the *interviews* rather than the *people* as symptoms of the complex First/Third World unequal relation.

But this is no neutral film-making practice. In the interweaving and sometimes contradictory strands of images and sounds are set the terms for a passionate commitment to a change of consciousness over First World assumptions. As in the moments when the missionary, assured in her conversion of the labour force to Jesus and to 'fear the Lord', whose voice extends over the travelling shot of appalling shanty town squalor to return on-screen in silence, baffled by a query about the lost self-sufficiency of those in her charge. Or as when the voice of the aforementioned agronomist traverses the 'natural beauty' of the plantation, advising the unseen film-makers of the 'best' time of the day to film; at that moment, we realise with a start that the images of women up to their waists in muddy water come from the 'worst' period and are thus forced to wonder 'worst for *whom*?'

Pineapple's mixture of history lessons, personal testimony and breathtaking images is complex but strategically key to the task of teasing apart the tangled strands of global domination. Barbarous pressures fuelling labour migration, acts of land piracy, national economic and cultural disenfranchisement, support for military dictatorships in return for commercial favours – all are evident products of early imperialist 'adventures', bound up with missionary zeal, colonialist enterprises and international commerce in a complex of overbearing forces. *Pineapple* reinterprets lessons from Latin American radical cinema of earlier generations and, in a more negative sense, perhaps also from the Godard/Gorin oeuvre (do the Burundi drummers pounding away at intervals in the bowels of the soundtrack echo the whispering voice of opposition in *British Sounds?*), to investigate anew the politics of this international landscape. On the basis of *Pineapple,* Amos Gitai shares with Raul Ruiz responsibility for a new dimension in counter-cinema, drawing upon celebrated Third World oppositional film-making practices in an assault on a smug First World consciousness of global economics and lazy documentary forms. Gitai offers a novel and liberating direction for future film essays. *(Framework* no. 29, 1985.)

Ananas

5 BANGKOK BAHRAIN

Michael Eaton

Country/City: Less about the places in the title than the movement of labour power through them, a movement in which Bangkok is not a starting point, but a middle term. The movement starts in the Chiapong region of North-East Thailand, the poorest part of the country where most of the recent migrants to the city came from. The film treats several different patterns of exploitation: the exploitation of peasants by landlords who operate the share-cropping system; the exploitation of the urban proletariat, particularly of female workers who, like their counterparts in Victorian England, must slip between roles of 'seamstress' and 'prostitute' after their arrival in town; the exploitation of Thai workers by the job agency operators who demand substantial amounts of money to secure jobs in the Middle East; the exploitation of Third World workers in the construction sites of Bahrain, where they are denied all residential rights while they save money to return to their native villages, completing the circuit of exploitation: Chiapong to Bangkok to Bahrain and back again.

Tourism/Labour: The first person interviewed is an ex-pat North American, explaining the changes in Thailand since it served as an R and R centre for soldiers fighting in Vietnam. War as the vanguard of tourism, producing a new service industry which now caters to the sexual fantasies of tourists from Europe, the States and Japan.

The second person interviewed is a bar-girl whose mother sold the family's buffaloes to raise the money for her daughter to give to an agency so she could work in Saudi Arabia – the money wasn't enough, so she remains in Bangkok. The poor travel to seek employment – the rich travel to seek new sensations, dragging the detritus of their culture in their wake. The world is re-made in their dark image, in the hoardings advertising James Bond films, in the fast-food joints, the topless bars of Bangkok.

Rich/Poor: The first of the exploiters to be interviewed is the owner of a work agency who was formally the chief movie censor. One of the films he cut was *Emmanuelle,* a film whose jet-set exoticism firmly associated the Far East as a backdrop for the sexual re-education of upper-class Europeans.

A Thai worker in Bahrain tells how he was jailed and given eighty lashes for drinking whisky.

Inside the grotesque opulence of a Bahraini boss's home a room designed like a Bedouin tent is illuminated by a chandelier whose size would not disgrace Versailles. The mirrored ceiling of the bedroom reflects the huge bed shaped like Cleopatra's barge with naked women carved like figureheads on its prow. A menagerie of furry toys crowds the nursery.

A Thai worker tells of his friend who sent money from Saudi to support his wife while he was away. He returned to find she had spent it and divorced him.

He went back to Saudi.
The poor work to remain poor, not to get rich; a bar-girl says, over images of a shanty town: 'I work for men. I work for money. Same you.'

Spying/Revealing: It is through such simple but none the less telling juxtapositions as the above that the film moves. As in all of his films Gitai refuses the construction of the exotic – the peasant villages, the shanty towns, the construction sites, even the drinking clubs and expensive hotels, are all presented as places of labour, not of tourism. There is a concomitant refusal of emotionalism in visual style: the characteristic hand-held camera, the almost empty travelling shots from the windows of planes and taxis; these techniques refuse *la belle image*. There is also a refusal of emotion in relation to the framing and questioning of interviewees: there is no 'psychology of exile' as in, say, Berger/Mohr's *A Seventh Man*, there is none of the double-edged prurient wallowing in the grotesque excesses of the rich as in, say, *Whicker's World*.

Like *Pineapple*, his film about commodities, Gitai deliberately, perhaps even fearfully, avoids any demonstration of identification with the people he talks to – he refuses engagement with the surface in order to attempt a revelation of the more abstract realities which underly and determine that surface. This approach, it does not have to be stressed, is very rare in documentaries which are interview-based and without commentary. It is indeed in the very distance he keeps from his interviewees, exploiters and exploited alike, that allows them to emerge, not as either people with problems or as nasty bastards, but as figures interpellated in a complex and abstract movement of international capital.

This is the effect on the viewer. One cannot help speculating, however, whether the effect on those filmed is very different in essentials from any encounter with a Western news or documentary crew. Whilst the editing and the structure of the finished film bends over backwards to avoid the voyeuristic, can the shooting, which seems to be regarded by the film-maker as the gathering of material which will later be used to demonstrate a thesis, albeit a pertinent thesis, ever be anything but the usual documentary smash and grab?

Is it merely a (well-founded) fear of documentary, a persistent and superstitious belief that 'the camera steals the soul', that makes this viewer at least wish to have inscribed in the film text some indication of how contacts are made, what connections exist between interviewer and interviewee, what role the filmed have in the determination of how their image will be eventually exploited on the television screens of the Western world?

On the soundtrack at the end of the film is David Bowie singing 'China Girl'. Never as abrasive or aggressive as Iggy Pop's earlier version (where the singer sounded like a strung out GI on R and R, incapable of not damaging the world in his demented attempts to forget himself) the song nevertheless contains lines which have a resonance not only in relation to the West's appropriation of the East, but also, perhaps, to the entire project of what is called 'documentary' cinema – even a documentary cinema as stringent as Gitai's in its attempts to avoid the production of humanistic crocodile tears : 'You shouldn't mess with me, I'll ruin everything you are.' *(Framework* no. 29, 1985.)

6 ESTHER

Richard Ingersoll   Rachel Neeman   Tamar Meroz

Richard Iingersoll[*]:
The ruins of Esther: Towards a Theory of Open Scenography
I don't recall smelling the perfume of angels of hearing the flapping of their wings, but I had the distinct sensation that I had been pulled outside of my body, to observe from a hovering position, as the roof caved in from under me. I soon rejoined my body in a devastated shambles of rubble, roof beams, and several thousand nursery-grown plants below. This was not a movie but merely the preparation for one, and in an instant the scene, which had taken several weeks to concoct, disappeared into a magnificent column of dust that looked to nearby friends like a cloud of smoke or a bomb. The set, which was intended to be the hanging gardens of Queen Vashti, was ruined, and some of the other sets perched upon similarly dubious buildings were as a consequence declared off-limits by the municipality of Haifa.

This was a rather inauspicious beginning to the filming of *Esther,* yet in retrospect it was a fortuitous event since it forced us to improvise in a manner that was much more consistent with the intended spirit of the production. *Esther* was Amos's first feature using actors and a structured narrative, and in preparation he had tried to immerse the crew in Pasolinian method. There are, of course, obvious parallels: Pasolini making an uncomfortable version of the New Testament and Amos doing something similar with a story from the Old Testament, but I think the interest in Pasolini was less contrived than that. Pasolini had an inspiring technique of using real architecture and real people, without robbing either of their dignity and reality, and this was worth emulating. Perhaps the closest analogy to this kind cinema are the *tableaux vivants,* which in the medieval city were the ephemeral transformation of everyday people and everyday settings for the purposes of an agreed upon sacred narrative. The ephemeral aesthetic for Gitai working in the ruins of the 19th-century Arab quarter of Wadi Salib was inspired by 16th-century Persian miniatures. With their flattened, skewed perspective, these colourful scenes present a very minimal architectural structure of pavilions and tents, upon which to hang lavishly decorated carpets and fabrics and in which to situate puffed-up pashas and harem women dressed in billowy, silken attire.

At a time when the budget for the big Hollywood production can exceed the yearly Gross National Product of many poor nations, and a single movie set can cost up to $2 million, one could argue that there are ethical reasons for filming in ruins and using whatever the location possesses as the premise for an image with as little cosmetic intervention as possible. Of course, when the budget offers no alternative, one doesn't have to bother with such moralism! Very few films that reach a wide distribution would ever make one doubt that the purpose of this art form is to create the illusion of reality. It is to Amos's credit that from the start he has been committed to a cinema where illusions are one thing and reality another.

That such artistic integrity has not been rewarded with mass approval and wide distribution is the logic of a society governed by illusions.

I had come to Haifa two months in advance of the crew to work on the locations and affect the minimal alterations to the four or five principal sites where we would be filming. The limits of the budget immediately involved me in the political reality of Israel. I could only afford to hire two Palestinian day laborers, who came to Haifa every morning at 7 on a bus from the West Bank, and left every afternoon at 2, working for a wage that could only perpetuate their subaltern condition and provide little incentive to do good work. They helped me clean, paint, and add vegetation to several sites, but communication was quite ineffectual, and it was always the case that just as we had reached a good rhythm of work, they would have to go home on the two o'clock bus. Fortunately, this is what occurred on the day the roof collapsed. Amos had come in the morning with his mother Efratia, camerawoman Nurith Aviv, and the great lighting and photography specialist Henri Alekan to inspect the set. There was a lovely little dome in the immediate backdrop of the set and beyond it the power lines and buildings of a more modern reality that would remain as a subliminal reminder of our times. Alekan was the only one who was skeptical about our artificial garden, believing that it was too cramped. The set was not yet ready when the Palestinians left that day and I continued by myself until the afore-mentioned disaster struck.

As I was waiting to have my shoulder reset in the Bat Galim hospital, amused at overhearing the Israeli doctors conversing in Italian (they had trained in Bologna and were nostalgic), I reflected on my misfortune and realized it was truly a blessing: what if the Palestinian workers had gone down with me and died, what if the crew, who was scheduled to film there the next day had gone down and the equipment too, what if Amos's mother went down? The spilt blood from my head and the ache in my shoulder were indeed welcome alternatives to those possibilities, but they did not reduce my shame at not having been more serious about questioning the structure's statistics. The set was in ruins, and although the idea of the film was to use relatively modern ruins to evoke the timeless realm of a fairy tale, these ruins were no longer accessible.

Amos, who even crosses the street with the certitude of a prophet, is brilliant in a crisis situation and quickly thought of alternative locations that were in fact better than the condemned locations. That major set, the palace of Avhashverosh, had to be relocated, and with the advice of Alekan, who made some lovely sketches showing the silhouette potential of domes and minarets, a vacant lot in the middle of Wadi Salib was selected to represent the palace: a grand palace without walls! This solution was indeed more attuned to the flattened space of the Persian miniatures. Carpets and pillows were strewn around the site, and a dozen flagpoles were placed symmetrically to give the edges some framing. Various buildings in the background were illuminated with coloured lights heightening the overall air of fantasy.

From that moment on, I must admit that I had very little do to with the design of the production, but simply tried to carry out whatever Amos, Alekan and Nurith wanted. My ambition as a set designer has collapsed with the roof, and I knew that this would be the first and last film for me. Yet the show had to go on. The 80-year-old Alekan had much to teach everyone. He was at once authoritative and modest, with a smile that constantly made one feel grateful for his presence. A good set has to be open, so that on one side the considerable spatial demands of the equipment-cranes, tracks, scaffolds, etc. can be accommodated, and on the other side so that the image can be sculpted by the lighting and lenses. If there is no room to move, it cannot be a movie. This is the first principle of openness in scenography, one derived empirically from a lifetime of experience, and one that is probably known to most film-makers. The other principle of openness, as we shall see in a moment, was spontaneously derived from working in ruins.

Due to the collapse of the roof, the first day's shoot was transferred to a site that needed little alteration: Mordecai's field. This was the only day the set was actually ready on time, requiring only some piles of stones and some bits of cloth to be tied to the branches of the trees; yet we still sat around waiting. Something just as calamitous as my roof had occurred: Simona, the young woman in a minor role, had run away! They spent half the day tracking her down and convincing her to return. Shy, with many doubts about whether she should be an actress, Simona's life had an uncanny parallel to Esther's, proving once again that life imitates art. Vashti's garden was moved to the seaside casino at Bat Galim, which had been abandoned when gambling was outlawed after the 1948 declaration of statehood. The scene was set on an open terrace about 100 feet wide and 200 feet deep. with an empty swimming pool in its midst. This indeed was openness. Vashti's platform and canopy were placed in the empty pool and we spent the whole day trying to fill it with water, but as it was cracked we were forced to keep the water running until the shoot was over much later that night. Alekan suggested we put bits of mirror into the water to pick up the lights. By late afternoon the breeze of the incoming tide strengthened violently and in no time had knocked down the canopy, breaking some of the wooden poles, tearing many of the drapes and sweeping them all over the terrace. The wind finally died down by the time it was dark and, instead of a hooded canopy, which was beyond repair, we improvised a draped screen, that was actually less restrictive to the camera's view that things that look right in one's normal perspective vision tend to look tighter in the viewfinder. Using some rough boulders, we had jerryrigged a path through the pool to the platform for Hagai, the chief eunuch, who was to enter three times with messages for Queen Vashti. Unfortunately, after many takes, the more the poor man repeated the scene the less stable the path became, and on his final trip (the take that was used) Hagai pragmatically waded through the water, much to the amusement of all. This is the sort of accident that gives *Esther* its charm. As almost every scene is composed of a single uncut shot, real time and the uncontrollable aspects of reality are consequently more present.

The choice of Wadi Salib for most of the locations was intended as a political subtext for Israelis. Here, in the middle of a lovely Mediterranean city on a slope between the flourishing port area and the business district of Hadar, was a once beautiful Arab neighbourhood, with some of the most architecturally distinguished buildings of Haifa. During the 1948 War most of the occupants abandoned their homes and fled to Lebanon. Subsequently, the municipality of Haifa allotted the buildings to immigrating Algerian Jews, who were given squatters' rights. After years of neglect, lack of basic services, and economic discrimination, the new residents of Wadi Salib made demonstrations in the 1960s which were met with brutal police repression. The troublesome Algerians were evicted from the neighbourhood and relocated at scattered sites; the buildings were then bricked up and left to rot. To preserve the area would probably have brought up the touchy issue of property rights, yet it was a pity to see right in the centre of Haifa the finest late-Ottoman buildings falling to needless ruin. To valorize Wadi Salib as the mythical site of Ahashvarosh's palace was thus almost as transgressive as casting the Palestinian Mohammed Bakri in the role of Mordecai.

One can best appreciate the state of decay of the Wadi Salib in the throne room scene where Esther is presented to the King. This was an utter ruin, with very unlevel rubble-strewn floors, stubs of walls sticking out, bits of plaster falling. There is something absurd about seeing a King in such a setting, yet it should be a reminder that architecture alone is not sufficient to convey the image of power and authority: what underlines power is the position of dependent bodies in space. The obedient minions of the court of King Ahashverosh, theirs bodies lining the irregular terrain of the set, independent of the built surroundings, transmitted a convincing image of authority. This was the beginning of my understanding of the second meaning of openness in scenography: the openness to reality. Esther's story went on with the costumes and actions but the reality of Wadi Salib was allowed to enter into the scene in the same way that in everyday life one accepts the unpredictable vicissitudes of weather.

This simultaneity of the real and the fictive creates an interesting tension in its anachronisms. The intrusions of reality into the play, the honking of a car horn or the passing of a jet plane, were welcomed into the texture of the film. During a certain scene, when Wolf, the narrator, was reading the edict of the programme against the Jews, three American sailors walked by in uniform. While amusing at the time, it seemed too contrived to include in the final cut. On the other hand, the most flagrant anachronism, towards the end of the film during the execution of Haman, was retained. This occurred atop the beautiful Ottoman walls of Akko, where dozens of Palestinian children, probably future participants of the intifada, were gathered off the set to be the chanting mob. Most people love the idea of being in a film, but few are ready for the agonizing amount of time one sits around waiting. It was hot, they weren't getting paid, and they all began threatening to leave. Finally, when the filming began, they exploded with exuberant cries of: 'Death to Haman!' which were quickly transformed into cheers for their favourite football team, and they converged wildly into the viewfinder. For a moment there was a genuine feeling of panic that the scene was going to erupt into a riot. Reality had been allowed to puncture fictional time and even predict something of the future.

The openness to reality, a method that was arrived at in such an ad hoc fashion through the experience of ruined sets and working in ruins, culminated in the final scene. Although not in the script, Amos perhaps invented this scene in homage to some of the long travelling shots in his previous documentary films. It is a single shot taken from a moving car that follows in succession each of the principal actors, now out of costume. In the background one has an impression of the crumbling ruins of Wadi Salib and each actor tells a little something of their real life, intimating that there are a variety of interpretations to the story they have been portraying. The visual field is completely open and documentary reality has invaded the fiction, making it quite clear why it is necessary to keep telling the same stories over again.

* Richard Ingersoll was the Art Director for *Esther*.

Esther

Rachel Neeman: Amos Gitai's film, *Esther,* premiered in the Tel Aviv Museum, is the first attempt in Israeli cinema to make a relevant political interpretation of a Biblical story. In his documentaries, Gitai has dealt with Israeli-Arab conflict. Here, in *Esther,* he gives us a message which is not strictly one dimensional.

Against the background of the Wadi Salib ruins, Jewish and Arab actors speak to us in Biblical dialogues, and from time to time this realistic set is disrupted by a soundtrack loaded with contemporary noises. Mohammed Bakri, a Palestinian, plays Mordecai the Jew and Juliano Merr, the son of an Arab father and a Jewish mother, plays Haman, the Evil One. A eunuch standing at the entrance to a steambath sings an Arab wedding song and we also hear Esther's attendant intoning an Arab song. At a banquet in honour of Ahasverus, Hebrew and Yemenite Jewish songs are played while the Queen and her attendants wear Indian saris. Gitai says that he chose the story of Esther because he found in it an almost archetypal thriller with typical heroes: the good, the bad and the beautiful – a minimalistic story. This is also the only Biblical story where God is not mentioned, which helped make his point: a protest against the excessive use of power.

At one level, the film is a statement against the historical lesson learnt by the Jews, who were once a repressed minority and are today a repressive military presence. 'They are persecuting an innocent people', cries Mordecai in Wadi Salib. But the casting of an Arab actor in the role of Mordecai the Jew introduces a new dimension, and with it an even more original comment: when the oppressed Palestinian refugees become independent, they too will go through a similar process and discover for themselves an object for oppression. The transition from oppressed to oppressor will not spare them and Mordecai, in Gitai's film, is not only the present day Jew but also the future Palestinian.

The landscape of Wadi Salib brings the spectator back to contemporary association; it focuses on a desperate situation and gives the feeling of a dead-end historical process. Outside, in the open stone locations, the film constructs an almost natural setting for the king's throne or the queen's bedroom. Here Gitai is probing a relationship with the orient in a place where the two Semite languages, Hebrew and Arabic, meet. Simona Benyamini, the actress playing the part of Esther, could easily be, by her looks, an Arab princess; the Bakri-Merr-Benyamini triangle is a visually harmonic triangle which further emphasizes the idea that the struggle is about power, not ideas.

The exotic images of the film, as well as the passive role of the camera, the importance of the text and the Brechtian elements such as the inclusion of a clown-like narrator (Schmuel Wolf) bring the spectator back to the medieval trilogy of Pasolini and particularly to *One Thousand and One Nights*. Although Gitai stays close to the biblical text, he doesn't present a strictly melodramatic interpretation of the story and thus saves us from the shallowness of an epic such as *King David*. The simplicity and minimalism of his sets also add several layers to the story. Beyond the ragged flag you can see the Wali Salib ruins, telling us that we are here and now. This is an interesting experiment on the cusp between documentary and fiction. And at the end of the film, Arab and Jewish actors tell us something of their personal histories and, in doing so, link the old myth to modern history. (*Koteret Rashit*, 2 April, 1986.)

Tamar Meroz: This is the Esther of Amos Gitai, a political film about persecuted people (who learn how to oppress) and unnecessary revenge. *Esther* accurately retells the Biblical story but does so in a new cinematic language of associated cultural connections beyond the merely visual. The Biblical text is read in accurate modern Hebrew, 'in the sound of the present day language', Gitai notes. Susa, the capital of King Ahasverus's kingdom (5th century BC) is located in Wadi Salib in Haifa. The place is both historical and contemporary and serves as both interior and exterior. The King's palace is found in an open field facing a minaret. Wadi Salib is loaded with socio-political associations and here the message is strong. The background ruins are not just seen by our eyes but also strike our memory. Internal synchronisation is at work here (Wadi Salib was a dense Arab quarter until 1948 and the stage for the riots of Moroccan Jews in the late 1950s). The actual stone walls cut across the classical narrative plot. The old stone decor stores memories which interrupt the story line. At the end of the film, the actors step out of diegetic time, cross the time barrier and tell their own stories. The dialogues are taken directly from the Biblical text but are pronounced in different accents and interwoven with Yemenite-Jewish and Palestinian songs. At several points the dialogues are not spoken but sung according to liturgies of Jewish prayers. The present day sound of the city is left on the soundtrack since the film doesn't take place in acoustic isolation. From a distance one can hear sirens of ambulances or police cars, airplanes are passing through the night skies of Susa and the panning camera notices parked buses and tourists pouring out to look at the ruins. This duality remains throughout the film as a counterpoint: the stylised Biblical plot and its metaphoric value for the here and now.

The construction of the film is based on Persian miniatures. Henri Alekan's lighting transforms the ruins into an architectonic system of shapes and visual symbols in which the characters play their roles. The scenes are often filmed in sequence shots where the relationship of the protagonists to the land changes from long shot to close-up. The camerawork was done by Nurith Aviv.

The film not only provides a deliberate alternative to the notion of 'the *Bible* now' but also that of 'Cinema now'. It uses realistic settings instead of the artificiality of studio reconstruction and is the first Israeli film to create a sort of Brechtian texture. The film is open to interpretation in terms of modern times. In a contradictory way, this film is patriotic, showing by its existence that Israel is a breathing and kicking civilization trying to innovate in the cinematic form without imitating other countries. (*Ha'aretz*, 27 March, 1986.)

7 *BERLIN-JERUSALEM*

Philippe Garrel

Amos is a poet.
Amos' film is sublime. Its women are more intelligent than the men, as in a film by Jean-Luc Godard. The camera follows a choreography, as in the films of Wim Wenders. It will become clear that this is the work of a dove aimed against the eagles.

It begins in 1920. Some Western emigrants buy fields from the Arabs and set up the first collective. In the evening, around the table, one hears things like 'You don't have to be crazy to be Zionist, but it helps.' And then, in a more unifying vein, working in the purchased fields: 'As long as there are no Jewish thieves, there is no need for Jewish guards.' In parallel, in Berlin, the newspaper writes that an arms cache has been found and that several Jewish resistance members have been arrested. Arms and resistance: why? It is now 1930 and Nazis begin to raid cafes, to spread tracts and to terrorize Germans Jews. In Israel, the response to the aggression is to arm themselves too. Now, fields left fallow by the Arabs are taken and quickly brought under cultivation. In order to be

a new jew who works the land there is no longer any need to buy it from the Arabs. There is a sense of urgency. For the pioneers, escaping from persecution and arming themselves becomes a necessity. It is said that 'Judas will rise' and, of course, the public here will have difficulty swallowing that, but over there, they say that's how it is.
In fact, it isn't like that all. From the outset, Amos films the face of a woman, a German woman, in big close-up. Now she is in a cemetery and says: 'Little one, you have gone back to the angels' and at that point the film takes off because that woman is a poet and is isolated from the others by her energy. Amos too is a poet, and isolated. Afterwards, she says to her lover: 'Keep dreaming' and she leaves. She passes by an autodafe. Someone says: 'Look, there's one of them', by which we understand: a German Jew, but one could just as easily understand this to mean: an artist, a communist, an anarchist, an intellectual and so on, as in Adolf Hitler's *Mein Kampf*. So, she makes haste. She buys a one-way ticket. Arriving in Israel, stepping out of the boat, she is really disappointed (yes, just like Daniel Cohn Bendit when he arrived in Israel), because Israel is a last resort, a little 'prefabricated' people would say today. Funny. And that's where Amos is really strong. Soon he gives her the lines: 'There is too much hate in this country. Jews and Arabs should understand one another.' We are in 1945. The woman is a prophet. But today, in 1990, Amos is also a prophet who has chosen pacifism rather than the wise men of Zion. (*Libération*, 14 March, 1990.)

Berlin-Jerusalem

8 GOLEM-L'ESPRIT DE L'EXIL

Markus and Simon Stockhausen   Marco Melani

Markus and Simon Stockhausen[*]**: Notes For a Diary** (10 July, 1991)

Monday, 18 February 1991
... another call from Amos: 'Tomorrow is the screening of the film. Can you both come?'

Feb 19th, 5.30 start from Cologne. Autobahn. 10.00 Paris, St. Cloud. Sunny weather, a drink in a small café, spring feeling, we are still early.
11.00 Some people are late. Around 12 o'clock we see the film. While seeing it we jot down our immediate ideas, feelings. Also we record the film on our video 8 camera. Later, in a little restaurant near the studio: discussions, doubts... Finally we decide 'to do it'.
15.30 in the sound archive: We copy sounds and ambiences from the original sound tracks – there are more than 120 tapes – for possible sampling processes. Intuition counts.
18.00 Odyssey through Paris trying to find the studio where Amos is cutting the film.
19.30 We see the whole film again. Talks. And again we see it, not without stops, questions, detailed comments and suggestions by Amos.
23.00 Drive back to Cologne. Heavy fog in Belgium. 4 o'clock in bed.

20 Feb. Markus sick, but the work starts. We see the film on our Video-TV. We develop 'themes'. For Hanna. Death. Tour Eiffel. Naomi. Boaz. Etc.
We record many sound tracks 'live' while seeing the film. Sometimes Simon's computer helps to prepare structures.

23 Feb. After four days' and nights' work our music is almost ready, only the ending is open.

A week later, 2nd of March, Amos comes to Cologne for two days. He sees the film in our home studio and listens to our music. Comments, suggestions, discussions. We re-record some of the material and finish it together with Amos. He takes the original tapes to Paris, on the 4th of March in the afternoon.

Later... contracts.

Later... Telephone call by Amos: 'New sequences have been shot.' Simon prepares additional music from our previous ideas.

4 May. Simon travels to Paris. Motorbike ride with Laurent [Truchot] to the

Champs-Elysees Studio. Two days of intensive sound mix. Rivka prepares good food. Amos looks terribly 'wasted', but happy.
Only two-thirds of our music remain. Less is more. The pictures are strong, and the music makes them even stronger.

Amos' approach to rhythm, density and balance is similar to our approach to music. He also loves the irrational as well as the precise, just as we do. That is why we can work together. Thanks, Amos, and good luck for your film!

*Markus and Simon Stockhausen provided the music for *Golem-L'Esprit de l'Exil*

Marco Melani: A Voyage to Moab to Witness the Birth of a Golem.

Amos Gitai, the Israeli cineaste, is a wanderer twice over: as a Jew and as a filmmaker. In Paris, where he has lived for a number of years, he is currently finishing his latest film. Its title has not been decided yet [*Golem: The Spirit of Exile*, Ed.). *La Goutte d'or* (*The Drop of Gold*) could not be used because its already exists. Perhaps *Nomads*, but on the clapperboard, below the names of the director and of the cinematographer (Henri Alekan) it says *Golem* because this is supposed to be part of a trilogy Gitai wants to devote to the mythical creature born in Spain at the heart of the Jewish diaspora-culture around the 12th century. According to tradition, it is a clay statue brought to life by means of a magic formula from the cabbalah in order to help the Chosen People during the persecutions suffered in exile. The elder brother of Frankenstein's monster and the father of all the robots and cyborgs of modern science fiction, the golem went from medieval Spain to the Prague ghetto, from legend to literature (in Gustav Meyrink's famous gothic novel of 1915 and more recently in Isaac B. Singer's children's story) and finally to 'the haunted screen' of the expressionist German cinema, first in a version directed by Henrik Galeen in 1914 (no longer in existence today) and then in Paul Wegener's film of 1920 which deposited the hulking figure with its slow, mechanical movements into the contemporary imaginary.

Amos Gitai's 'monster', in contrast, has the soft and sensual features of Hanna Schygulla: a female golem, mysterious and seductive (see also the Langian mechanical heroine of *Metropolis*), neither nasty nor terrifying but positive, fertile (like only a woman can be) and who does not rebel against her creator but ends up recreating him. Besides, the creator is not the old rabbi but Vittorio Mezzogiorno in civilian clothes. However, although adapted to the contemporary world of workers and immigrants, Gitai's film is just as mythical as its silent predecessors. In its own way, it is a mythological, metaphorical, metaphysical film.

The incunabula of Paris
The production's bus takes me straight from the Charles de Gaulle airport to the set, the already mythological location (at least in my eyes) of the immense area on the metropolis's periphery where they are building the new library of Paris. When

they tell me where we are, the vision of dinosaur-like machines and of cranes lifting entire metal walls into the sky is overlaid onto my memory of the slow, endless tracks through booklined corridors shot by Alain Resnais in the old library (the new one will replace it) for a marvellous little Borgesian documentary, *Toute la mémoire du monde* (1956).

The bus descends right into the cavernous depths of the huge foundations and there, on the fresh earth, Gitai and his crew are preparing the next scene. In the face of this gigantic factory, working day and night without interruption, the cinematic machine which so often appears unwieldy and cumbersome seems minuscule and quiet. Sparse and busy, the handful of people around the clay puddle looks like one of the clouds in a Leger painting. 'When I went from documentaries to narrative features,' the director tells me, 'I basically retained the same artisanal approach: a crew of five people, one of them managing the production (on *Ananas,* that person also recorded the sound). It's all very intimate. I prefer it like that. The heavy structures with dozens of people on the set bother me. This way, I have the option of changing things even at the last minute.'

A few shots are taken of the general environment: the digging, machines in operation, the city in the distance. In a little while, the place will have lost its current connotations: it will have been buried under slabs of concrete. There will never be any 'false returns' to this set (return visits to the archaeological sites of cinema like Lisca Bianca, the island of *l'Avventura*). There is something thrilling about photographing a space that is about to be transformed, which will leave its only and fragile trace on celluloid. Gitai is like Rosselini amidst the ruins of Italy in *Paisà*.

This is the last day of preparation and they are shooting the beginning of the film, a sequence shot. A small dolly runs on some ten meters of track. Firmly holding onto the camera, Agnès Godard is pushed back and forth by the grips while she tries out the framing. I have never seen her come off that perch before all the takes are in the can, in spite of the icy cold wind. The great Henri Alekan (about 80 years old and who has worked alongside Gance, Cocteau, Carné, Genina and, more recently, Losey, Edwards and Wenders) arranges for the whole thing to be lit; his faithful chief electrician, even older than him – admiring whispers suggest he is 92 years old – discretely carries out the instructions. Shooting will commence at dusk. Meanwhile things are being tried out; preparations are made.

By the light of the setting sun, Vittorio Mezzogiorno, dressed for the scene (a thick cotton jacket and muddy plastic boots), marches off by himself amongst the piles of mud like an engineer supervising the work on a building site. In fact, he is concentrating and repeats a long and complex monologue: the text of a magic formula. Gitai's explains: 'For the cabbalists, the secret of making a golem is in the Sepher Yetzira, a kind of cabbalistic grammar which regards the letters of the Hebrew alphabet not simply as elements of the alphabet but as the very fabric of creation itself. The word is extremely important in the myth of the origins.' Hanna Schygulla has been closeted for hours in the make-up trailer: it isn't easy to change oneself into a clay statue.

In the meantime, Amos Gitai wanders around the set supervising his collaborators' work, calm and a little mischievous, like a cat about to eat a mouse. He certainly is not one of those directors who maniacally control every detail. He appears much more interested in the elaboration of a complex set-up than in it's execution. He projects, the others implement. Like Rossellini and the Renaissance theories of Leon Battista Alberti. Over and above his concentration on, and feeling for, space (qualities he had since childhood, his father being a Bauhaus architect and having studied architecture himself in Berkeley), Amos Gitai is first and foremost an architect of cinema, mainly through his way of working.

And I, what am I doing here amidst so many busy people? I was invited by the director and by the Italian co-producers (Camilla Nesbit of Nova Films). I am not part of this grand array of internationally famous people who participate in this stateless film: the film-makers Samuel Fuller, Bernardo Bertolucci, Philippe Garrel and Marceline Loridan, the French actresses Fabienne Babe and Mireille Perrier, the Spanish Marisa Paredes, some of Peter Brook's African actors, two of Pina Bausch's dancers (Antonio Carallo and Bernard Levy) in addition to Hanna Schygulla and Mezzogiorno. It is an extraordinary role call of directors. As for me, I don't even have a walk-on part. I don't have to perform, only to observe. I am a witness, an eye, a look. Perhaps one of the critic's last incarnations is that of the detective who observes and questions (himself). If so, then I too am dressed for the part: when I disembarked from the airplane I put on a Marlowe raincoat.

The Birth of a Golem

'In the beginning, the golem is merely a massive lump of clay to which a human form is given,' Amos Gitai noted in the introduction to the script.
    The troup is gathered around a waterfilled claypit. All along its edges there are unfinished attempts at mud sculptures: some have a recognisably human shapes, others are no more than formless heaps. One of the shapes is almost complete. Manzu had done something similar for Adam and Eve in Huston's *The Bible*. The dolly runs parallel to this theory of inert fetishes. Night has fallen and it is dark now.

'Essentially an obscure, dark mass, the golem presents itself as a rough and ready body animated by a pure fire. That is why the myth of the golem really is a myth of light, of enlightenment. What is the golem if not a substratum of deffered light?' (A. Gitai, idem).

Alekan arranged his lights on top of an embankment to obtain a 'moon effect'. There is a weak, bluish light striated with expressionist shadows. The director says: 'As for the lighting, we are working in the tradition of the great German films.' The camera is on the dolly, looking down on Vittorio Mezzogiono, following him while he goes from one mud statue to another reciting the cabbalistic formula with Wellesian gestures, like an illusionist. In the end, the magician-engineer stops by a body, half submerged into the soil, in a foetal position. It seems to react to his words, it moves; it stands up.

Hanna Schygulla's body is covered from head to toe in a brown, earth-encrusted bodystocking, a mud-filled wig on her head. Her face is white. She stands up, slowly and gracefully, with puppet-like movements. The creator 'helps' her stand up by reaching out to her but without touching her, his hands just close enough to caress the air around her.

'Michelangelo's fresco showing the birth of Adam is the starting point for the scene where the Maharal animates the creature and gives it life. The image refers to the gestures chosen by the painter in order to evoke the breath of creation.' (A. Gitai, idem).

The sequence shot, from the long shot of the night to the close-up of the actress, is captivating. The moment when the golem begins to move is thrilling. Hanna Schygulla's acting evokes a creature that is a cross between a woman and a serpent. A fantastic creature which simultaneously attracts and frightens us.

'Why', I ask the director, 'a female golem?'

'For me, female characters are always more interesting, like Esther or the characters in *Berlin-Jerusalem*. Besides, there are other female golems in the Spanish cabbalist tradition of the 12th century. Hanna Schygulla embodies the spirit of exile invoked by the Maharal to come to the aid of Ruth and Naomi, the real heroines of the film. It is a maternal and a creative golem, not a destructive one at all.'

9 *METAMORFOSI DI UNA MELODIA*

Edoardo Bruno

The Long Road

Amos Gitai's cinema is like a long journey ranging over things and people, town and countryside, panoramas and landscapes. The idea of movement, rooted in Hebraic culture, underpins the choice of roaming through past and present telling Biblical stories and old legends. It is the bridge – the load-bearing element – which holds history and poetry together. It is the way an engagement comes to expression, finding ancient, almost oracular accents in a form of mental architecture. Exile, the search for a homeland beyond the current confrontations are the sign, the mark – from *Esther* and *The Golem* via *Berlin-Jerusalem* – of a cinema grounded in its very materials, its ideology fusing with its form, light, speech, sounds.

In *The Golem*, Paris, as the land of Moab, is a space segmented by continuous tracking camera movements or surveyed from atop image-arousing cranes, the camera's mounting and descending routes tracing a specific network of trajectories, a dynamic geometry. The death of Elimelek (Sam Fuller) and his funeral make up the elements of the myth, recalling archaic figures engraved in the sacred attitudes of a gesture of love. Earth, water and air make up the claylike material of creation and the myth of the Golem is re-imagined in terms of The Wanderer in the land of exile, a metaphor for a nomadism in a state of continual transformation. In this way, the urban and the archaic landscapes are brought into conflict. The death of the father in the city and the birth of a child on the bank of a river become symbols and allegories of a story that has become part of nature itself. *Esther, Berlin-Jerusalem* and *The Golem* form an open-ended trilogy, an extended fresco of the long journey of the Biblical diaspora on the way towards utopia, holding out among the ruins of the destroyed cities, an epic of deracination traced through many generations. Persecutors and the persecuted chase each other dialectically in circular figures, conveying the obsession of a mode of thought pervaded by ambiguity. It is no accident that for Benjamin ambiguity is the fundamental feature of allegory.

In the theatrical work, *Metamorphosis of a Melody*, presented in Gibellina (Sicily) in July 1992, Gitai pursues that same obsession through the staging of Flavius Josephus' *The Jewish War*. Formerly the leader of the Jewish resistance against the Romans, Flavius Josephus, when captured, became the historian of that very same war. 'This', says Gitai, 'is the root of his ambiguity: he does not want them to cut off his head, so he turns traitor, but at the same time he cannot resist a certain feeling for the Jewish side. The oscillation between reason and emotion is felt in every line, and there lies its fascination.'

The ruins of a town destroyed by an earthquake – old Gibellina – buried under an enormous catafalque of concrete, have all the power of the original Hebraic setting. Burri's monument, fascinating and terrible with its whiteness, traces an ideal geography of the destroyed land, its streets re-drawn, which Gitai, attentive as always to visual and sound values, accentuates through lighting and by sending motorcyclists through them. Gitai approaches the monument like an ideal projection inserted into a typically Israeli mountainous landscape, moving his actors across this territory of the dead: Sam Fuller, Hanna Schygulla, Jerome Koenig, Masha Itkina and Enrico Lo Verso. We perceive in the play of light, illuminating in turn different fragments of the scenario, a sense of cinema: a restless, increasingly intense sense of the relationship between things and memory, between suggestiveness and rigour. The siege of Jerusalem, the desperate resistance, the Roman forces hurtling in on their motorbikes, exerting a power of intimidation with their violently noisy impact, are the material embodiments of a mental construct, of an allegory of an historical event that is also acutely and deliberately present. Betrayal, violence, terrorism, resistance, in a conceptual metaphoric form, converge in an image-evoking representation which still sustains the sign of a geometry of motion, of the journey.
The music of Markus and Simon Stockhausen, Masha's laments, the songs of the fishermen, the metallic sounding rhythms of the blacksmiths, the sounds of the wind are woven together into a distant echo of ancient legends. They form the sound fabric corresponding to that representation on 'the big white screen', the image-symbol of a story that repeats itself.

Translated by Judith Landry

Amos Gitai in Gibellina

PART III

GITAI ON GITAI

1. ON DOCUMENTARY AND TELEVISION

By launching a rather successful kind of investigative radio journalism, and then applying similar methods to television broadcasting, the BBC established a form which has come to dominate all other ways of representing 'reality'. Today's television presents an almost homogenised documentary form. This characteristically consists of showing a sequence of images covered by a narrated commentary which tells you what you should see in those images, eliminating the possibility of the viewers making their own sense of them. It also frequently incorporates a series of frontal interviews – again based on the radio format – which provide information, a collection of supposed 'facts' delivered verbally. The resulting exclusion of all other documentary forms presents a serious problem, specifically because television is such an important medium for documentary. It dominates our perception of issues, of problems, of other places, of the way we see the world around us.

I'm much more for a form of documentary which asks the audience to do some associative work. Instead of frontal interviews I prefer to choose a sequence of documentary situations – by which I mean sequence shots containing interaction, arguments and contradictions – events as they are captured by the camera. I then connect these situations in a way which makes sense, which constructs the larger whole of the film. Even working in this way, it is always easier to proceed according to certain formulae, for instance according to geographical proximity or to chronological sequence, or to construct an argument of some sort. I think we should break these equations and do something which would relate places or fragments of biographies and construct a different understanding of the way people live and the issues involved. This calls for continuous innovation in creating other ways of telling a story.

You use fragments of biographies, recorded sounds, documentary situations, and you attempt not to edit images and arguments out of their context, eliminating the use of a strange voice in the material. When some information is missing which is crucial to our perception or understanding of the situation, I prefer to print it on the frame as a written text rather than in a commentary. I would rather make it as clear as possible that this information comes from somewhere else. It is not a sound which mingles with the other sounds recorded on location, but a text printed on the frame, explicitly shown as supplementary information.

I've noticed in documentary films a kind of hierarchy in the identification of interviewees. A manager of a company is identified if interviewed, but a worker may not be. I don't accept this kind of hierarchy, so I just identify interviewees by their positions. Also I'm not interested in personal attacks or personal praise. I wish to show the structures in which people operate and which oppress them. This also helps to balance the fact that the films themselves generally deal with very specific stories. That is another distinction I would make between my approach and the reportage method. I find it difficult to make a film about an issue. I would rather try to define a specific story or sequence of memories which reflect an issue. I couldn't do a film dealing with the Palestinian-Israeli relationship just by collecting statements by Begin, Arafat, etc., and putting a commentary over shots of refugee camps and houses in Tel Aviv. I would rather show a very restricted story about a house, and the transformations in the ownership and social relations of that house, so that the memories of people, which at times seem almost irrelevant to our specific story, could be constructed in turn to describe actual personalities taking part in a larger conflict.

I have had many discussions with intelligent producers within television, and they are always weary of the internal wars they have to wage to allow different kinds of film to be shown. I don't think that because I don't like some of the films on television, or the forms it generally uses, or even the very instrument itself, that the site should be abandoned. Even documentaries, when shown on television, are seen by a considerable number of people, and it is important to show people other forms, other attitudes, other sorts of political approaches, and other ways of portraying a situation. I have found in many cases that it is as difficult, or more difficult, to convince television producers to show another form of documentary as another point of view.

Maybe it was for that very reason that *House* was prevented from being shown on Israeli TV. The very fact that it shows people from 'the other side' as three-dimensional human beings is a way to counter official propaganda because you see them as complex as they are. It's easier to have the propaganda machine rolling when everything is reduced to two dimensions. Perhaps the censors were threatened by the way the Palestinian worker in the film expresses his emotions in poetic and complex language, because this runs contrary to the view of some Israelis that the Palestinians are 'primitive'. In other words, those who decided not to let the film be shown were more worried, maybe unconsciously, by this challenge to their prejudices than by the direct content of the film. A Palestinian worker talks in a complex and sophisticated manner while a well-educated professor of economics at the Hebrew University, the Head of the Advisory Board to the National Bank of Israel, talks in poor and primitive language.

2. ON PRODUCTION

Before making a film, I do research in a very factual way. I try to understand the places we are to film in, to get to know as many things as possible – the foreign exchange rate, the economic situation, very journalistic things – and then some of the literature and the mythology of the country. But when we actually film, this is not something to which I constantly refer back. I try to relate to it while we are working, but I don't have a notebook and insist on asking questions I've already written down. You have to be very 'tuned' when you are filming, and this takes a lot of concentration because people sometimes give you a sort of jewel – they reveal something you didn't know or they express it in an incredibly compact way. In *Pineapple,* we gradually discovered the role of religion, which wasn't in the preliminary concept of the film. More and more we found people in the role of missionaries. Before you introduce economic colonisation you have to change the way people perceive reality. In the film there is a conversation with a missionary in the Philippines, who explains how people once believed that when a person dies and you hang the body from a tree, the soul will go to another person. But now they are made to believe that all the souls go to the church. So there is a sort of bank of souls, a central institution, and they have to accept the notion that they should keep on good terms with the central institution.

I think that generally one makes a film for oneself and for a loose group of more or less like-minded people, unless the film is a purely commercial venture. When I make a film, I don't have a narrow commercial purpose in mind because I feel that there is no point in doing so. I would merely be pandering to what is anyhow a system of illusions. I have met all too many film-makers who have insisted on telling me that the compromises they made in the last film would enable them to make the *real film* next time. That's hokum. I'm interested in what my sensibility, my vision, my feelings have to say at any given moment and that's it. I don't cut until I'm satisfied that nothing remains in the shot that ought to be seen. It's very subjective. Film-making is a very subjective process. When I look at a moving image there comes a point when it no longer interests me. That's where I cut. And I do believe that my films are indeed understandable. I know very well, though, that it requires a degree of focussed attention on the part of the audience. And nowadays that's considered cruel and unusual punishment! I feel very strongly that such a trend should not be indulged. The media have accustomed people to such a flow of repetitive information that attention often slackens – I'd say almost in self-defence. Anything worth saying will sometimes demand a little bit of effort from the audience.

3. ON CHARACTER AND NARRATION

One of the themes that always interested me, both in the documentary and in the fictional films, is that of characters who move between opposites. I want to explore the range of the inner contradictions in which they act or play, and the way that they manage to survive in such complex situations. People who came here from Eastern Europe and others who came from Western Europe, from North-Africa or from other places, brought with them different cultural identities. What happened to these people when they were confronted with the difference between their world and our particular reality? In what way was their sense of identity affected or transformed? One of the curious things about the history of the Jewish people is precisely the dialectical condition in which they managed to survive so many centuries. It is the life story of people who lived in a certain given geographical environment but prayed and longed for an 'other place'. The period of Ben Zakai, with the destruction of sovereignty by the Romans, is very interesting in this sense. At that time, a big effort was made to endow all the institutions and the rituals of the state-structure with abstract meanings. For instance, with the destruction of sovereignty, agricultural state holidays were transformed into abstract non-territorial memories. The Holiday of the Trees ('Tu Beshvat') was in April because that was when the almonds blossomed in Jerusalem. In April, Jews living in Poland, when the land is still frozen, would look at a bunch of dry raisins and say: 'This is the Holiday of Nature'. Such memories with physical, sensual and particularly geographical origins were transformed into total abstractions. The twentieth century, which brought the creation of Israel, caused a radical transformation in the perception of these memories which were elaborated through centuries of existence in the diaspora. The desire to jump over nearly two thousand years of exile with the choice of Hebrew and its revival as a living, modern language, after it had been restricted to liturgic texts and prayers for hundreds of years, those are the issues and the elements which interest me. I'm trying to relate to some of these themes through cinema . In general, one can say that the film-maker is confronted with two forms that have to be addressed at the same time: the first one is the shape of the theme and the second one is that of cinematic form. For the Israeli film-maker, the former is naturally attached to dealing with the Israeli-Arab conflict, a subject that for a long time had a kind of taboo attached to it. Even today, though more film-makers are referring to the subject, it is still largely neglected in the cinema. As a generalisation, one can say that the Israeli cinema is by and large still mired in the clichés of narrative melodrama, using cinematic forms adopted from other countries. It would be difficult to find here an attempt to invent and develop a form that would be appropriate to the specific conditions of this country. The strong, overwhelming attachment the Israeli cinema has to the American cinema cannot but be wrong for a country which has to evolve some particular cinematic solutions to its own kinds of problems and conditions. A small country like Israel with a population of four million Hebrew-speaking citizens is in itself a restricting element as far as commercial distribution is concerned. I think it would be rather useful for the Israeli cinema to refer to the Middle-East and to the mediterranean region as a whole. You cannot avoid the question that cinematic form has by itself a political dimension. How can we create a critical cinema while at the same accepting the colonisation of the cinematic language by referring all the time to the style of American melodrama?

There are certain advantages to making a film now, at the end of the 20th century, rather than fifty years ago. Not many, but some. And one of the advantages is that some of these things have been shown already, over and over again. And unless you happen to want to make a film that is just full of cliches, you have the option of referring to these things. Your audience knows the cliches, so you don't have to repeat them. You can make a reference to an existing sequence of images, to something everybody already knows about, and you can construct out of this maze of connotations an epic story.

4. ON CLOSE-UP

A close-up is an exclamation mark in cinematic language. But you don't want exclamation marks all over the place. Sometimes you want to say: just look at the ruins and the artificiality of the situation. The characters in this story [*Esther*] are walking amidst ruins – and yet you believe me when I tell you that this is a palace. You accept the axiomatic truth that this is a palace. But it's actually a ruin – and if you're an Israeli audience you will recognize Wadi Salib and be aware of the historical connotations. But in the midst of this mood of distanciated contemplation you do occasionally want to highlight a point with an exclamation mark, though you will only want to do this sparingly. The narrator's entrances and exits are obvious instances – so you use the exclamation mark and he looks straight into the lens, in defiance of the golden rule of traditional cinema that actors must never look at the camera. In oriental art generally there are few instances of close-up. Close-ups are somehow an invasion of privacy. They are an aspect of individualism. The Orient is not a great believer in individualism, which is a Western notion, and a rather modern one at that.

5. ON COLOUR

Since we know of the existence of certain Indian or Persian colour codes, [*Esther* asks] let us see what the relationship might be, for instance, between colour code and class in ancient Susa, green being the colour of the nobility, etc. Or let's gradually change the shade of Mordecai's attire, until eventually it becomes as darkly brown as the garments worn by Haman. Traditionally, colours have corresponded to a kind of social code, not only in ancient Persia. A similar phenomenon exists today: if you work for IBM you wear a special tone of grey and a distinct type of suit, and that is a kind of code. But I don't think that the IBM generation is necessarily the world's best judge of Persian colour codes.

When we were researching colour codes in Persian miniatures, I was greatly impressed by the way in which a single miniature can tell a whole story and explain both the context and the relationship between a number of characters in the action. In a way, this implies a cinematic attitude – and I mean this quite seriously. We built a tower on the set for a high angle shot of the location and one could almost have painted a miniature by observing the elements within the frame.

We spent several weeks making more precise drawings of [*Esther*'s] sets.

The set designer, Richard Ingersoll, was quite surprised that so little construction work was required. We decided that the thing to do was to add bits here and there, very gently. We also decided to keep the colours of Wadi Salib, the crumbling paint on the shattered walls, the blues and yellows and greys. There was no need even to clear away the weeds, because I would rather have them in shot. On the main set, the camera was positioned on a kind of plinth, and a lot of the 'decor' was actually structured by lighting.

6. ON ARCHITECTURE AND CINEMA

I was interested in the relationship between international architectural trends and its adaptation to the conditions of the Middle East, such as the climate, the wind, the sand and the other features characteristic of the region. I was also interested in the artisanal aspect of architecture. The beauty of old buildings is derived not just from their formal properties but also from the way they were built: slowly, moment by moment. It is no accident that one of modern architecture's main problems stems precisely from its excessive industrialisation, like the notion of prefabrication, the reduction of the structure to a design that then merely has to be executed.

The thought processes of film-making and architecture have a lot in common. When you make a film you have a subject or a story, and you have to make a shape out of it. Something else I like about both mediums is that they are not such intimate arts: there are industrial and social structures involved. So you're going through a long process of translating your idea through a lot of filters until you finally get the result. The main thing is whether the structure works: the building stands and doesn't fall, or the film exists. There's the spine, and the walls, and the beams – to continue this kind of metaphor – and you can see them but they don't interfere with the inner spaces of the building or of the film. So you have a structure which allows you to read into the building or the film, but it doesn't over-interpret the inner spaces: each one has a kind of cumulative effect, like when you walk through a space and each corridor or room or window gives you another vision of it, but you will know it's a continuous structure.

When I started, before I did architectural films, I did completely formless films. I needed a reason for my environment, or for myself to be making films, so I did some films about architecture. But they were very short, five minutes or so, and they were just looks, concentrated looks. Later I did some real films about architecture. Then I got a grant for another one, but because of the 1973 war in Israel, I wound up making *Ahare,* which was about war and memory. I asked the grant committee to approve it and when they did, that was the end of the architectural films.

Unlike modern architecture, cinema has preserved some aspect of the 'artisanal', of craftsmanship. When working on a film, anyone of the technical crew or in the cast puts their own imprint on the final work. Precisely this aspect has completely vanished from modern architecture due to its method of production: the moment an architect concludes the design stage, the plan will be executed and the opportunities to make substantial elaborations or improvements during that implementation are minimal. This is a rather new phenomenon in the history of architecture and building. A Greek village, for instance, was never designed centrally by an architect. It was the result of a long agglomeration of forms involving continuous negotiations between local master-builders. If you take a more hierarchical architectural structure like Gothic architecture, you will find that since the concept of the Gothic cathedral was shared knowledge at the time, many of the plans for these building were drawn physically on the building site itself in a 1/1 dimension. The actual process of articulating it into the specific architectural form was done in the very building process. The stage of creative activity was not concluded with the official design but went on throughout the entire construction of the building. This is one of the problems of modern architecture due to the radical transformation in the last century of the way architecture is produced. The work of some film-makers still evolves around this ongoing production-creation relationship. You have a script, fine, but then you have to make a film out of it. The lighting, the movement of the camera, the cutting, the set... all may drastically change the initial intentions written into the script. This allows you to link or to dissociate things that were supposed to be continuous, for instance between the definition of the palace of the King in the text of *Esther* and the actual decor of the Wadi Salib ruins, or between a very lyrical text and the noise of city traffic. You can reassess your options and your position throughout the process of film-making because you have the liberty continuously to link or to dissociate what are presumed to be axiomatic relationships. Summing up, one could say that in today's architecture builders literally have to execute the pre-existing plan while the film-maker can reevaluate his position at every stage regarding the choice of colour for the costumes or the choice of set, of the decor, the casting and so on. The problem for cinema is that today it is coming closer and closer to the ways of modern architecture.

    The story chronicled in the *Scroll of Esther* happened in ancient Persia. It is probably the only diaspora story included in the *Bible*. I found it interesting to take this story and film it in Israel, referring to the contradictions inherent in the fact that this diaspora story is filmed in 'the homeland'. This is something that also interests me in architecture. For instance, isn't one of the charms of Tel Aviv, a modern architectural work, that it is one of the outcomes of Herzl's dreams? Isn't this charm related precisely to the very fact that the city is a failure of a great theoretical idea? Tel Aviv isn't just another shtettl on the shores of the Mediterranean, very human, warm, utterly non-utopian. Here we find perhaps one of the strongest experiences of the twentieth century: the spectacular process of the collapse of an ideological mammoth and of grand expectations. In some ways it is a rather impressive experience. This great idea which nourished the last hundred years gave people a sense of hope, but the desire to put it into practice in such a hermetical manner has led directly to its collapse. That is why we built a dual time structure into *Esther*. The film is shot in a semi-classical 'decor' and is spoken in biblical Hebrew. But the decor of Xerxes's great palaces is the site of the ruins of Arab houses in Wadi Salib in Haifa. On the film's soundtrack you hear car noises, ambulance sirens, everything which characterizes the sound of the

Israeli city. So on one side we have the agglomeration of elements which create a continuous fictional story, on the other side elements which break apart the classical quality of the story and throw it back into the Israeli reality of 1990. *Berlin-Jerusalem* has similar elements. That film ends also with a sequence shot that brings us gradually from the 1940s, the period in which the film takes place, to 1989, when the film was made, like when someone signs a text and puts a date on it when it is finished. The complicated sequence shots with which I like to finish a film functions in the same way, registering the time when the film was made.

The Romans destroyed the entire temple of David in Jerusalem and left only the Western wall. When you observe this wall vertically, you see traces of different conquerors. The wall really is a very powerful symbol because of its abstract quality. The top is from the Turkish period, further down it is from the Arab Mamluk Empire, further down you can see the Roman's touch, below that you see Herod's time – big arches – and still further down there are remains of the period of Solomon and so on. So you have a kind of vertical map on which the whole of history is represented in an abstract manner. It is a very effective fetish of 'history'.

7.   ON THE *BIBLE*

The stories of the *Bible* have always appealed to me, especially those of the *Old Testament*, because the characters are never portrayed as perfect human beings. There are no angels and no flawless individuals. They all suffer, they all sin, they all do things they know are wrong, and the *Bible* registers the contradictions of its heroes. Take the story of David, for instance. He is a very powerful King, in many ways a model, and yet he is a sinner: in order to indulge his love of the beautiful Bathsheba, he sends her husband off to the front to be killed. The story of Job even goes so far as to question the very existence of God. He says: 'I am just and yet I suffer while there are cruel and corrupt people who are wealthy and lead an easy life. Where is Heavenly Justice?

8.   ON ISRAEL

In a sense the Zionist dream is a success story. Yes it is, because it has managed to construct the State (and that was the essence of the idea) with all its institutions. I think that when ideologies drag on too long their vitality evaporates. The real urgency is lost. The Zionist dream was vibrant when the situation was urgent. It achieved its immediate aims. Now the original dream is no longer a driving force, because it is a reality. The Promised Land has a flag and a national anthem. It is no longer a dream but a tangible entity. Only a new sense of purpose can meet a new challenge. And now there is a generation which must come to grips with a new and urgent situation to find in this very complex region a set of solutions that are livable. This requires a new dream, as fresh and ardent and innocent as that dreamt by the pioneers. Israel can survive by political agreement. We must recognize that the great myth has achieved quite a lot and that now comes the time for finding ways to resolve the very harsh conflictual situation instead of merely holding on to the status quo. We can dream of peace. We can dream of constructing the Middle East. I don't know if these are things we can actually achieve, but at least they are not bad dreams.

9. ON VIOLENCE

It is very risky to be too realistic in this kind of film [*Berlin-Jerusalem*]. I haven't seen many scenes of violent conflict on the screen that are really convincing. Very often the violence is so overstated that it loses the nightmarish quality it has in real life. Very few film-makers can convey violence authentically. Maybe it is because most of us are merely acquainted with violence, not familiar with it... One of the ways around the problem is to try to construct a poetic representation rather than to go for social realism.

Amos Gitai and Henri Alekani on the set of *Esther*

10. ON LIGHTING

Henri Alekan is an exponent of that great classic period of the cinema which was so ferociously attacked by the New Wave with their predilection for what they liked to call 'realistic lighting'. The incredible skill of constructing space with light was neglected for years and few people nowadays have it. Henri Alekan is one of those great traditional cinematographers who learnt their craft with very insensitive stock and had to work out ways of creating different layers of light. I was very happy when he agreed to work on the film. I think it was also important that someone from a more modern school did the operating: Nurith Aviv is herself a cinematographer but in this case she agreed to do the camera work. As you know, the sequence shot is a very complicated thing to get right.

Every time I work with Henri Alekan, I like him more. It is always a different experience. He is young, open, vivid and different in every film. For *Esther* we used a lot of filters. It was shot completely on location and for the night shots we used projected colours to transform the places. To *Berlin-Jerusalem* he brought an expressionist element to the lighting, a linear kind of lighting. We approached *The Spirit of Exile* as a series of tableaux, not in the expressionist manner but more like the compositions in Flemish paintings, Vermeer, Rubens at times. The colours are much more subdued, yet much more articulated in each image.

It's a matter of finding the right balance, just as for the text. Alekan is not in the least dogmatic and he possesses an enormous amount of knowledge, which is fascinating. He knows about certain ways of lighting which very few people remember nowadays.

11. ON SOUND

There is a theory I rather like, which says that at some point a film starts to fight for its own soul. The film keeps certain people out and keeps certain people in. It becomes a kind of independent being, and I like that thought. So Antoine Bonfanti happened to be a friend of Laurent Truchot, the production manager, who has been crucially important on this film, and one day Bonfanti came by, looked at the short treatment, which was all we had available in French, and after only half an hour said: 'I'll do the film'. It was a great pleasure to work with such masters as he and Alekan. The kibbutz sequences were very tricky for Bonfanti because we were not far from a working quarry, operating 24 hours a day. He had tremendous sound problems. He is the sort of person who would go about stalking sounds like a Mohican, and whenever I didn't see him for five minutes, I knew he was out there listening to the place. He would find spots where the surface of the earth was not quite flat but had little bumps and would hide microphones. He never stopped for a minute.

12. ON MUSIC

A friend of Nurith Aviv's had noticed [M. Stockhausen] playing trumpet in a classical concert in London and suggested him as an actor! We did not imagine he would also write the music for the film. One night when we had finished shooting the scene [of *Berlin-Jerusalem*] where Else runs downstairs during the book-burning, Markus, who plays the part of her young lover, stood on the bottom of this immense staircase and played his trumpet. It was about midnight. Everybody was very tired. But it was so beautiful that we all just stood still. Bonfanti ran to his Nagra and started recording immediately. At the end, Alekan looked at me and said: 'Fabulous!' It was obvious that Markus had to do the whole music score. The theme is simple, piano and trumpet, and I find it both strong and moving.

13. ON POLITICAL MYTHS

The first of my censored films, *Political Myths* is a documentary without any real narration. What frightened them was the material showing the Betar festival with its echoes of Italian fascism and the young man who talks about building a new Jewish race. It reminded me of the *Bible,* of Moses facing the Golden Calf. In the *Bible,* two notions of religion confront each other. That's what Straub brought out so well in *Moses und Aaron.* When he comes down from the mountain, Moses wants to found an abstract religion, not territorially specific but a religion first and foremost based on a very strong morality. In a way, the Gush Emunim and the Cisjordanian settlers who tend towards a territorial notion of religion, where some places are more sacred than others, use religious terms to defend a new kind of pagan faith.

Reading the *Bible* (the Old Testament – not the New one, which is only an edifying text) always fascinated me and quickly led me to see the world in terms of sharp contrasts. It is a book bursting with conflicts and the characters, even the most positive ones, have their dark sides. Take David, one of Israel's most important figures: in order to seduce a married woman he has no hesitation in sending her husband to the front to die.

This film continues the themes of *Charisma* and *Dimitri,* that is to say, the relationship between political or artistic performance and so-called reality: concrete, documentary reality. *Political Myth* is one of the films I built up by way of "capsules": sequences with their own self-contained stories and contradictions. I had a friend who was a conceptual artist, Avital Geva. He put bits of calves' heads on the "green line" which marked the Israeli border before 1967. It was a reference to the story of the golden calf, a reflection on the relationship between fetishism and the occupied territories. It was also a reaction against that kind of vulgar religiosity that sees Judaism as something physical, something territorial with borders. I filmed his performance and he talked about how Moses burned the golden calf and dispersed its ashes to destroy the power of material objects. That was one of the capsules. The other one was about the rituals of the right, of Begin's party. The affiliation rituals for new party members had a lot in common with those of Italian fascism: the invocation of glory and pride, jumping into a fiery circle, and so on. The third capsule deals with the members of a religious youth movement which invokes Massada, talking about glory, death and suicide for honour's sake. Massada was where, after a long siege, the population committed mass suicide in order to avoid falling into the hands of the Romans and becoming slaves. Massada is a very important symbol for today's Israeli state because it represents an act of rebellion, of pride and dignity while at the same time celebrating suicide.

That was the first of my films which Israeli television decided not to broadcast. They asked me to re-edit it, to cut it and so on. There were many rather bitter discussions and in the end they didn't broadcast it.

14. ON *BAIT*

Israeli Television did not want to admit that Palestinians have memories, attachments and rights in this part of the country. Such a recognition would mean, on a political level, that a political solution must be found for the Palestinians, not just as individuals but as a people. The version that exists of the film is in fact the one before the final cut, because the man responsible for the documentary department in TV came into the cutting room and demanded that I stop work immediately. Since my previous film had already been censured and later even disappeared completely, I had taken the precaution of making a video-tape which I sent abroad.

Roughly the structure was as follows: a house becomes the scene where different characters come and recount fragments of its history. Each intervention corresponded to a new phase in its construction. Gradually the entire structure of the building, of the film and of the conflict emerged. Before making *House* I wanted to make a film about a machine and the people who used it. These people would come and recount fragments of their biography. The machine's functional operations would have tied the different stories together. The machine creates relations of production but a house evokes human relations.

In the property registers, the names of previous owners, that is, of the Palestinians, have been erased. The labour government didn't sell the house, they only rented it to Algerian Jews. But in 1970 there was pressure to sell these properties, to privatise them. We had to find out who the successive occupants had been and locate them. The most difficult thing was to trace the Palestinian owner.

The workers were filmed on the last day of shooting. They resisted and didn't speak. The last day, we got the impression they wanted to unburden themselves, as if to get rid of that pain. For them, building a house on top of an old one is bad. In a few years the house will collapse. It is an Arab house and it will remain so. That is the idea at the heart of the resistance.

15. ON *WADI*

Wadi is the optimistic counterpart to *House*. On the margins of society it is possible to coexist. The Arab couple (Palestinians) and the Jewish brothers from Rumania (Israelis) talk in complementary ways about their previous and present situations. The starting point is the same for both of them: they are all refugees. The third couple, an Arab and a Jewess, don't give any so-called political information, but they portray mainly the way they relate to each other on a personal level. In their case I left out all information that would have told you about their objective situation. Stylistically I wanted to achieve a very static effect: three couples thrown together in an isolated area, in a forgotten hole so to speak. Their very fragile memories reflect their living conditions. I didn't want to show the individual people too specifically in their own living quarters because I wanted to maintain a certain level of abstraction. I didn' t want to tell the story of a particular place, but that of a particular situation. In *Wadi* the two Jewish brothers each tell of two separate events: one happened a few days before we began filming. The police came and beat them up because they had fired shots in the air to scare away what they thought were thieves. The other story dates back 40 years and is about the time of the concentration camps. The two stories get disastrously mixed up.

American Mythologies

16. ON *AMERICAN MYTHOLOGIES*

It is a fairly abstract documentary. I didn't want to link the various shots with a narration pointing out the things you are supposed to see, the things I think you should see. It is more a montage of visual and aural fragments which represent America for me: a very brutal society with a few people on its periphery trying to behave like human beings, underlining the general thrust of the film. It's a very commercialised culture. You can't use a classical dramatic structure to portray a disintegrating society because what holds a disintegrating society together is precisely the associations, the residue of old stories: stories about Indians, hippies, about the sixties, old traditional American stories, all gathered together on one terrain. All of them together, that's American culture.

For the second part of the film, we went to an Indian reservation in the North East, near Seattle, where on one side of the bay there is the reservation and on the other side is the Boeing factory where they make those gigantic planes. On one side you have supertechnology and on the other, the survivors of an old culture living in caravans and mobile homes. If you want to portray that kind of reality you have to accept ecleticism. You find leftovers of strange things right next to each other. There are different forms of telling a story. You can tell one in a very didactic manner, always making sure that everybody understands your intentions each step of the way. The problem with this form is that unless the story is really unique, or tells something extremely new, you are understood after the first few minutes and it becomes boring to follow the didactic exposition of what you have said in the first few minutes. The audience is not actually offered anything new to observe, except reiterations and more illustrations of what has already been said. ~This is especially the case when dealing with some elements of American culture. American culture is an abstract theme: there is nothing particularly physical about the subject. So the form of the film has to be abstract as well, because the form relates to a particular content. You cannot make such a film in the same way that you would if two guys were going to Nicaragua with a camera to try and follow a revolution. It has to be in a different form.

It is no coincidence, really, that Joyce wrote *Ulysses* after some pieces of reality disintegrated for him, or that Bellow is composing a juxtaposition of African and modern civilisation. This is the phase of culture we all live in, so it would be quite anachronistic to use a documentary form which would indoctrinate us with all this, as if it all cohered effectively. That is like telling a different story, because it just does not fit today.

If you try to look at 'American Culture' in the 80s, you don't find any coherent movement, such as, let's say, Dada in the 20s, or a collective of artists working and thinking together. Instead, you find very powerful individuals. You find Jane Fonda; in architecture there is Philip Johnson;
a few powerful personalities in the fashion industry, the media and so on. These powerful individuals are extremely eclectic. They collect elements from their environment. Philip Johnson collects styles. Parts of his new buildings are copied from the Galleria in Milan, others from a Gothic cathedral. The style is then called Post Modernism – another new trade mark for a new authenticity. Jane Fonda collects a piece of a radical speech from Berkeley, another piece from some other place, then she repackages it and redistributes it very forcefully. The Punk fashion designers, who are already established, do a similar thing: they take a swastika, which used to mean certain things in a certain context, and rubber pants, a red handkerchief, they package it all together and redistribute it very forcefully, with the media, music. So if you want to generalise, I would say that the culture itself is in a process of disintegration and shows non-coherence: ecleticism of the past without any clear movement for the present. So the form of the film had to be broken to express this. It could not be made with a coherent form.

When you understand how these individuals operate – the production of stars – you start to see the systems of control in the US, the way stars are used in the systems of control and the use of fashion and of culture in general. On the surface, when you look at the US, there seems to be no structure, but there is a very clear structure of control. To some extent that is what we tried to show.

17. ON *FIELD DIARY*

In this diary of the occupied territories I wanted to examine how violence against the Palestinians is "legitimised": violence against their belongings, their land and against their very existence as a people as well as individuals. The film's theme and atmosphere are laconic. The banality of evil, the destructive occupier's lack of conscience and his self-justifications. It is also the story of the occupier's inability to face up to his own actions, taking refuge in abstractions (God, the Nation, Security) and turning that into a mechanism for legitimising what he does. I wanted to deal with political events in such a way that some of the roots of the problem can be understood. This is the political meaning of the film. Since the subject, occupation, is not a very cohesive reality, I looked for fragments with which to demonstrate this, trying to examine how the occupation manifests itself, and to understand the mechanism by which people explain to themselves why they are occupiers. It was known for half a year that there was going to be a war in Lebanon. Sharon wanted an excuse to go and have a war. Excuses were found when they shot the Ambassador in London. Sharon, the Chief of Staff, and others kept saying that there really was a military solution to the Palestinian problem, or specifically to the PLO problem. That meant going to Lebanon because the PLO was in Lebanon. It's not such a big secret. When we invaded it was quite clear that the purpose was to annex the West Bank.

We started filming three months before the invasion. The Begin-Sharon scenario was already quite clear: in order to annex the West Bank they had to destroy the political base and the military base of the Palestinians in Lebanon. The weakness of the whole argument, if you analyse it rationally, is that they cannot change the basic components of the conflict unless they decide to exterminate the Palestinians. If they decide not to exterminate the people on the West Bank, if they were only to annex it, then fifty per-cent of the population would vote for Palestinians for Parliament. Begin would no longer be Prime Minister. In *Field Diary* we were looking at the escalation of violence, the mental build up for violence. You know Golda Meyer said that the Palestinians did not exist. In *House* I was dealing with the most basic facts: the Palestinians have attachments and memories, relations to a piece of land. This too carries political meaning.

At a certain point the violence reaches such a stage that it makes you feel like vomiting. Then you want to react. I don't have a machine-gun in front of me, but maybe I can have access to a camera. I don't want to use it as a machine-gun, it's a different instrument.

It is always quite interesting to examine the contradictions of a situation. What does Begin's speech in the desert have to do with the invasion of Lebanon? What is the role of myth and the ideological build up that Begin wants to make.

Why does he need it? Where does it come from? What is exploited in order to produce it? The past? History? The bones? You have to try to deal with the question in its context. The Lebanon invasion is not a separate event, it belongs to a larger context, it has a political purpose. Since the answers to these questions are elusive, we try to compose shots which are rather long and include some contradictions.

Field Diary is actually composed of very few shots, maybe fifty in the whole film. In most cases each sequence is one shot. The structure of the film contains a sequence of capsules, each of which is self-contained. You don't edit images or arguments out of the context of the unit. Each unit contains arguments, contradictions, imperfections, perfections of the shooting – events as they are captured by the camera. We can take this one step further by juxtaposing images with a sound that contradicts what we see. On the image of the destruction of the landscape I used the sound of a radio drama for Israeli children explaining the story of roots and attachments to land; or the Jewish death prayer over Lebanon. Each take is self-contained but at the same time the capsule makes a point, or several points, by the way it relates to the preceding or the following take. It is in this cumulative manner that the larger whole of the film is gradually created. In using this series of sequence shots, and in establishing a dialectical relationship between images and sounds, the structure of the documentary echoes the nature of the subject matter; it tries to capture the contradictions.

None of the shots were rehearsed, nor were they totally improvised. There was a concept and in some cases, like in the opening shot, I would guide the route of the camera. Whenever we saw a scene which was somehow related to the subject, we would shoot. It was like a net. There were things I wanted to touch. Many times I didn't know where or how a certain scene would fit into the whole of the film but if the associations were there, we filmed it.

For instance, my brother Gideon went to a refugee camp in the Gaza Strip which was under curfew. People in the camp told him that they didn't have enough food, so he went to a nearby kibbutz, Keren Shalom, and explained the situation. People of the kibbutz gave Gideon some boxes of tomatoes, cartons of cigarettes, bread and some milk for the children. He went back to the refugee camp and gave it to the people there. A man in the refugee camp was so moved that he walked to an olive tree, cut a branch and gave it to Gideon.

A few days later, the people from this kibbutz called and told me they were going to visit the Mayor of Nablus (who was under house arrest). I was still thinking of this olive tree story, so we went to Nablus and there was this incredible scene with the soldiers. When we finished, we put the camera in the car, switched on the radio and heard this radio drama for children about the pomegranate. I thought there was an association with what we were doing although at the time I did not see how it would fit into the film.

Geographically we concentrated on the same route around a number of fields. Most of the film was shot within a range of about 18 km. We would go from Tel Aviv to the Nablus road, then we would turn right and go north to Ramallah. We would come back on another road that passed these settlements and then tour through the Gaza strip. These were the two basic loops. For us, the traveller, the film-maker, the wanderers in these places, reality is a juxtaposition of different events in different places.

I think we should always look for a formal or a thematic solution to present a situation. If we don't find new ways to tell stories, then the media will fill this gap and produce a very superficial image. The media give us fragments of information, then they make a big drama out of these fragments. In this sense *Field Diary* was an effort not to deal with the political events the way the media portray them. If we examine the context in which the events take place, maybe we can criticize it better.

18. ON *ANANAS*

The pineapple has a kind of texture which makes it a better filmic object than, say, an apple. On the label of a tin of pineapple it says it was produced in the Philippines, packaged in Honolulu, distributed from San Francisco, and in the corner it says: printed in Japan. So, the pineapple can tell the story of the relations between workers in the Philippines, executives in San Francisco and the Pre-Christian civilisation of Mindanao. It can tell you how Christianity had to be introduced in order to homogenise the perception of reality. A missionary woman explained that they had to introduce Christianity, otherwise people would have taken the fruit from the fields, and that would have been stealing. So they had to teach people a sense of sin. Furthermore, the Christians could not accept that when somebody died, the native people would hang the body from a tree so that the soul could go to somebody else. That is too anarchic: it means that the soul itself can search where it wants to be embodied rather than having a central bank of souls like that of the Church. So it had to be explained to these people that all the souls have to be centralised first before they can be redistributed. Castle and Cook were two missionaries from Boston who went to Honolulu to convert the natives. They were also the ones who started the pineapple plantations.

19. ON *ESTHER*

In this trilogy I took a number of metaphors from our literary heritage and used them as a kind of raw material. Initially, I was preoccupied by two different kinds of Jewish mythology. On the one hand, there is the myth of suicide: the story of Massada where 760 people held out against the Romans until it became obvious that the only possible outcome was defeat and enslavement. Then they all committed suicide. The other myth represents the exact opposite. The story of Esther is a story about survival, about a group of people who are persecuted and choose not to commit suicide but to fight back. They use all the means at their disposal, and above all their intelligence, in order to survive.

Another aspect I found interesting is that it is the only *Bible* story where God does not play an active part. I was also attracted by the sheer beauty of the story, the minimalism of the biblical text. And so I decided to use the biblical text and dialogue literally. It took me quite a long time to work out why I was so attracted to the story of Esther and what its meaning was in terms of today. But when I looked at it more closely, I realized that it is about a cycle of repression. It is about oppressed people who gradually turn into oppressors.

There are winners and losers, but the *Bible* insists on the contradictions of victory. The present-day situation in the Middle East is somewhat similar. People who were persecuted not so long ago learn to persecute. That in turn confronts us with a circular, ongoing tragedy which is relentlessly rooted in the *Bible*. Both sides keep referring to the ancient texts in order to justify their part in the conflict. The story gradually becomes more and more bloody and intractable. In the story of Esther, there is no way out. The situation is utterly claustrophobic.

The myth of Esther is very strong and very present in Jewish memory. Purim, the feast commemorating the story of Esther, has been celebrated through the centuries by Jews in many countries. It held a magnetic attraction for people suffering endless persecution and who could not help hoping that eventually a time would come for revenge... But obviously revenge brings with it contradictions, in that the recently victorious become obsessed with power. Strangely enough, the actual ending of the story tended to be played down, even omitted altogether. When I asked some of my friends, it turned out that all of those who knew the story of Esther could not remember the real ending. It has simply been wiped from the collective memory.

I thought I should look somewhere into ancient mythological material and find a fairytale story rich in metaphor. Formally and artistically, I needed other ingredients and subject matter to work with. That is why I decided to build my first feature film upon an old text. The problems of keeping the balance and the proportions right seemed a very interesting, real challenge.

Esther

The film was shot in the ruins of the old Arab neighbourhood of Haifa, Wadi Salib. Palestinians lived there until the 1948 war. Then Moroccan Jews moved in. In the late fifties, the Moroccan Jews rebelled. As a result, the Haifa municipality decided to disperse the population of Wadi Salib and destroyed the neighbourhood. And this area in the centre of the city has been left in ruins to this day, as a kind of testimony. If you want to cross Haifa, you have to drive through these ruins. Many of the founders of modern Israel were Europeans and that influence remains very strong. Yet there has to be a meaningful cultural dialogue in terms of the whole region. And what is intrinsic to this region? There is a certain sensibility, a certain light, the colour of the olive trees, the colour of the air and the stones, a kind of harshness... All these are elements of the Orient, and they have to be rediscovered in Israel.

Esther takes a certain concept of time and deals with it through a structure of detailed and articulated sequence shots. Each of these is so devised, that the actors are constantly on the move in relation to the camera. The design of every shot is constructed so that there are no edits within any one scene – each scene consists of a single shot. This approach generates a pace and a pattern different from the generally highly edited fast-moving melodramatic films. Moreover, the story of the Meguila (the biblical story of Esther) is similarly divided into chapters in the *Old Testament*. Each chapter or scene consists of a single shot, which contains the point of departure, the actors in motion, their dialogues recorded live, sounds related to the action and the intrusion of irrelevant city noises like traffic and the howl of ambulances, the hum of aircraft overflying the location, the rough and random shapes and colours of the ruins contrasting with the deliberate shapes and colours of sets and costumes... All of this – the irregularities alongside the regularities – is contained within each single shot.

20. ON *BERLIN-JERUSALEM*

I wanted to make a film about the mythology which sustains and pervades modern Israel. The mythology surrounding our pioneers is extremely powerful and shapes present-day attitudes in all kinds of ways. They are held up as examples we must try to emulate and we are constantly exhorted to be worthy of them. That's fair enough. But unfortunately, with the passage of time, their constant use as instruments of persuasion has worn away the distinguishing features of their individuality; the pioneers have become icons – still recognizable, but unreal. I wanted to restore the vibrancy of life to them, to wind them backwards, to liberate, as it were, the beautiful insect caught in its beautiful amber coffin. The pioneers were magnificent because they were human and not because they were walking icons. And being human implies doubt and fear and hesitation-depression too, and occasionally hopelessness.

The film is constructed out of the biographies of two women: one of the early Zionist settlers from Russia and a German Expressionist poet. It is a juxtaposition of the two, so the film moves back and forth between Berlin and Jerusalem, between these steamy cafes and the pioneers in the hills. Berlin was a fabulous city in the 1920s, very creative, and one of the reasons was that it was so open to foreigners: there were a lot of Russians and Poles, and Jews. In a sense, the real effort to deal with Modernism came in Berlin, not in Paris, which was still the outpost of bourgeois art.

Basically, *Berlin-Jerusalem* is a story of broken utopias, like a lot of my films. There's some kind of struggle, but also the helplessness of the struggle. Israel, and that's always one of the difficulties of criticizing it, is this kind of very long dream that the Jews have maintained under the most difficult conditions of persecution, anti-semitism, and so on, but once it's materialized, it has all the contradictions of any other dream or idea. In that sense, the Jews aren't unique.

Else Lasker-Schüler wrote a very beautiful play, her last, which is called *Ich und Ich (Me and Myself)*. The play was censored by her friends who would not allow it to be published for a long time. What she wrote was an apocalyptic vision of Jerusalem: she has Himmler arriving at Gey Ben Hinom, a valley near Jerusalem, and telling Mephisto to put some gasoline into the tank he is driving. In a sense, Jerusalem has become such a place, because everything is so mixed up. The centuries are mixed in such density. Jerusalem is a city where you can go to a church and it will be shared by fifteen different sects and they will have agreements about who can step on which stone and when. So in a sense, conflicts which sometimes involve great powers and immense territories are symbolized in minimalist terms in Jerusalem. The city bears witness to the creation of many things and also to their destruction. So I think this almost crazy eclectic final shot is about all that. The sounds and images of this one shot make a concentrated recapitulation of the entire film. It connects the wonderful innocence of the beginning to the collision of the utopias and I think it is the right ending.

21. ON *GOLEM-L'ESPRIT DE L'EXIL*

The Biblical text of Ruth is based on a documentary story: a family in Bethlehem suffers from the famine there and goes to Moab, the 'new country of exile'. But the Biblical writer takes this event and transforms it into fictional material. And this then becomes eventually even more than fiction, it becomes a sanctified myth. We, in turn, place the Biblical story in the present and work with those ambiguities, but we strip away some of the sanctification, keeping the mythological echoes but placing them in the here and now.

The Golem story was described throughout the literature of the 19th century as an industrial object which, like the industrial revolution would help humanity in its manual needs. This is especially illustrated by Gustav Meyrink's book and Leivick's play. In earlier literature, the Golem was an earth-like paganistic fetish. When I looked more closely at the story and read the texts of Gershem Sholem, I became more interested in the spirit of the Spanish Cabbala, which goes back to the 11th century. I felt closer to the interpretation given in the *Sefer Yetzirah, The Book of Creation,* which is supposed to have been written in the 3rd century, or even earlier. These are very early texts which relate to a kind of spirit, or body, which defended the nomads or the exiled in their wanderings. One popular story even says that the golem is *the wandering Jew*. When we constructed the role of

Schygulla, I was more inspired by this much more abstract embodiment of the golem than by the 19th century version we are all familiar with. The lines spoken by Vittorio Mezzogiorno and Hanna Schygulla at the beginning and at the end of the film are literally taken from *The Book of Creation*. These lines register the Cabbalistic idea that realities can be created by words, not only described by it. Reality can be brought to light by the use of correct combinations of letters. Borges said that the meanings of the Scriptures are infinite, like the hues in a peacock's tail. The Cabbalists would have approved of this view; one of the secrets they sought in the *Bible* was how to create living beings. They established Cabbalistic combinations which associate an organ of the body, a month of the year, a particular human quality and so on, and they tried to specify the relations between all those elements. They investigated the origins of creation in the most direct sense. The question of creation provides the frame of our film and inside that frame you have a permanent movement to exile and back. This is embodied by the story of Naomi. The relations between Naomi and her Golem, her spirit of exile, created the final form of the script.

Some argue that the *Bible* is supposed to have been written by men. But I find its female protagonists particularly interesting. In spite of the heavy patriarchal traditions which establish the role of the men, the women-characters are rather central to the text. In a way, women play a revolutionary role because they provoke the social order which is then settled by men. Men are the kings, the warriors. They impose a certain structure, an order. In Biblical terms, the role of women is to be the keepers of human memory. After all, the *Bible* is about memory, about keeping memory alive. It's about constructing a mythological text out of pieces of biographical stories.

When I fictionalise a mythological text, I'm also looking at the way any text which is not just a narrative is fictionalised. Obviously, we are living in a world which is becoming more and more homogeneous in terms of cinematic expression. We no longer have Pasolinis or Glauber Rochas or Rossellinis. Cinema is again quite an industrial form of production. Good films and less good films are more similar to each other now than they used to be twenty or thirty years ago. A kind of modus vivendi seems to have been adopted in cinematic language. In these three films I tried to deal with some of my own questions regarding the cinematic language. One of the things you find in these Biblical stories is a certain literary quality of symmetry and opposition. Here you have the initial couple, Naomi and Elimelek. They are succeeded by two sub-couples when their sons marry Moabite women. Then the father and his sons are killed and thrown out of the story. The dialectic of opposition is then in turn inherited by the two daughters in law, Ruth and Orpa. Orpa wants to stay in her own country, Moab, and enjoy life. She is not a puritan or a moralist. Ruth, in a great expression of solidarity, is willing to leave everything behind and to embark on a voyage together with her mother-in-law. They have a destination in mind: Naomi's country of origin. In the manner of mythological stories, later on, Ruth and Orpa will become grandmothers. Ruth's grandson is David. Orpa's grandson is Goliath. The on-going conflict between different human desires will continue. Essentially, the idea of working with this kind of minimalist dialectics attracted me when I embarked on this film project. The question of the transformation of these biographical stories into a mythological text is an interesting subject in itself.

It's my first film in French although I've lived in France for quite some years. Until now, I always found ways of doing films elsewhere and not dealing with France. I made films in Israel, in North America, in South East Asia. Then I shot *Esther* entirely in Israel. For *Berlin-Jerusalem* I shot some locations in France, but I chose ones which could stand in for Berlin. *The Spirit of Exile* is the first film where I try to address the place where I live, trying to make some sense of my relation to it as a *stranger*. You could say that it's autobiographical, but then so is everything else we do.

The Spirit of Exile is the third part of a trilogy, with *Esther* and *Berlin-Jerusalem*. It's the last of three films dealing with people moving from one place to another, being displaced in some way. *Esther* is a diaspora story where the persecuted become the new persecutors. Although the film *Esther* is actually placed in Israel, it is still a diaspora story even though Israel was built as an antithesis to the diaspora. *Berlin-Jerusalem* is about the question : what is the destination of Utopia in a century which was packed with utopias? The film asks that question in terms of the relations between different utopias, represented by the two main protagonists. In *The Spirit of Exile,* the central spine of the story is the theme of being uprooted, which is an on-going preoccupation in the entire trilogy.

As a film-maker, you have to find a way through a maze of cliches. I'd like to put it this way: is human civilisation constructed only by people who stay permanently on their own land, or are nomads also responsible for some of the great contributions to civilisation? It seems to me that many great human achievements have been created by people who moved from one place to another. It isn't all due to people who stayed in one place and crafted their own roots. The debate between nomads on the one side and peasants and city-dwellers on the other, seems to be a permanent fixture. If we take Berlin, the cultural centre at the beginning of the twenties, and you look closely at the people who contributed to what is now considered to be the German culture of the twenties, you will find Germans, and also Hungarians, Poles, Jews, Russians, Dutch, Indians, etc., a great complexity of people who jointly contributed to the art and the culture of the 20th century. This is the side of Paris I really like. In Paris, there are blacks, Chinese, Arabs, Jews, French, etc. All these variations contribute to the common culture. In the film we say: look at this civilization of nomads and the way it was presented in the old mythologies. Look at the way that these people move on the surface of the earth, creating poetry and texts as beautiful as the Bible.

We tried to include a number of people coming from different countries, bringing a variety of accents; most of them do not use the French language in the classical way. Neither do they use a kind of natural, 'very cool' language, which at the moment dominates French cinema. 'Cool French' is not very open to immigrants. Generally one can say that there is a growing negation within the 'cool French cinema' of the existence of people from other cultures. You hardly find any immigrants in any substantial roles.

Golem – The Spirit of Exile

In this film, the Spirit of Exile itself, embodied by a female Golem, is played by Hanna Schygulla. She has a German accent. The creator of the Spirit of Exile, the Maharal, is Vittorio Mezzogiorno, with an Italian accent. Boaz, a kind of Biblical nobleman, is played by Sotigui Kouyaté and he uses a Malian accent and sings in African languages. Naomi is played by Ophrah Shemesh, who brings Hebraic influences. I think that some film-makers are exiled in a way, even when he or she lives in his or her own country. You need to have distance from your own reality.

Actually, the film's two heroines do not want to be part of the discourse that certain racists are engaged with. Obviously, racists enter into arguments because they want to be heard, they understand the methods of intimidation. So they use provocations to become visible. And the two women are not keen to respond. If you look at the attitudes of immigrants, most of them are quite defensive. They like to keep a low profile because they feel semi-clandestine, even when they are natives or when they have passports or residence permits. They never know what stratagem will be used next to kick them out, so they try to stay away from conflictual situations. They don't feel they are on their own ground. I wanted to treat these kinds of timid reactions of the two women as a sort of survival strategy. There is an affinity between them. They feel very close to each other and they want to preserve this kind of intimacy in the face of this world. That's also why they don't enter into battle against the rest of the world. They want to preserve their voyage. As a process of transition in their long journey together. It is a sort of a conceptual voyage in which one will always remain a nomad, a soul in search of its own identity.

Cliches are sometimes very useful because they are also very ambiguous. For instance, when I did my documentary *Pineapple,* all I had to do was say the word 'pineapple' and all kinds of associations opened up: exoticism, a fresh drink, the light of Hawaii. I like that kind of fetish that provokes all kinds of associations. The same goes for the Eiffel Tower. We shot inside the metallic structure, sometimes you recognize it but at other times it looks like a cage. The fetish becomes an abstract cage that captures the characters. Part of the question is: where are the modern rituals?

22. ON *THE WAR BETWEEN THE SONS OF LIGHT AND THE SONS OF DARKNESS*

The Jewish War by Flavius Josephus is an account of the destruction of Jewish sovereignty and of the first Jewish city, Jerusalem, in A.D. 70. At the same time, it is probably the oldest journalistic text on record. Josephus collected testimonies from warriors and generals, and synthesized those with statistics of the period, texts from India and so on. Before becoming a historian, Josephus had been a leader of the rebellion against Rome in the Galilee. He was captured by the Romans and was left alive on condition that he would write the history of this period. I suppose that the Romans knew what they were doing when they got Josephus, a Jew, to tell the story of the victory over the Jews. They knew that in order to glorify themselves, they had to glorify the people they conquered. But, as always, the surprise is that the individual has a capacity at times to be careful, cunning and intelligent enough to register information that he or she wants to pass to other generations without the people in power being totally aware of what's happening.

Josephus was a very talented writer and his text preserved for us the material as well as the intellectual existence of the period. Politically, Josephus was for *real-politik*. He opposed the suicidal manoeuvre of the zealots at Jerusalem and he told us the story of the destruction of the city as if the zealots had brought it upon themselves.

The Massada story is about the suicide of seven hundred women, men and children. They decided to die rather than to become slaves of Rome. Modernity recycles many of the old myths and the Massada mythology is one of them. It had been totally forgotten for centuries. The diaspora was not interested in a suicidal mythology. These people had to concentrate on surviving and keeping a sense of identity in very difficult circumstances. But when the Jews returned to Israel, archaeology became part of an important national effort to reassume legitimacy, to create a pre-text legitimizing the contemporary state. One of the most fabulous sites they dug up was the fortress at Massada: a completely isolated mountain in the middle of the desert. After Jerusalem had fallen to the Romans, Massada had continued the rebellion. To survive in the face of the Roman Empire, the people in Massada found ingenious ways of getting water from the dew of the desert, of building irrigation systems, finding ways of storing food, and so on. The Romans had already destroyed most of the country and exiled massive parts of the population, but they were obsessed with this tiny country, Judea, and the Roman generals went back just to conquer this insignificant mountain in the middle of nowhere. This disproportion in the Massada story made it an excellent myth for the new state to grab. In the early years of statehood, the famous phrase 'Massada shall never fall again' became a slogan.

But in a way, Massada is too pure a model. Focusing on it exclusively makes things really simple. Hollywood understood that when they made a very successful television series about the Massada story. What happened in Jerusalem was far more complex and allows an insight into a great ideological battle. The irony is that three hundred years after the Romans exterminated the Jews in Judea, the whole Roman Empire converted to a religion that had started in the very country they had wiped out. These kinds of contradictions are fascinating.

In the plays [in Gibellina and in Venice], I wanted to put interrogation points into the main text without mixing them into Josephus' text. So, for instance, Hanna Schygulla recites a text by Oscar Wilde, 'Each man kills the thing he loves', which makes a comment on Josephus's very heroic text about Massada but also about the attitude of the Romans. In most of my films you can find that kind of dialectic. You have the surface of the text and then there is a figure like a narrator who puts questions onto that surface. When we presented *Metamorphosis* in Gibellina, Sam Fuller's role was inspired by that of Flavius Josephus as the story-teller, the narrator. There was always some light on Fuller and he was very close to the audience. In this way, the audience could look back at him which he was reporting on the battlefield behind him.

The play establishes a kind of dialogue between blocks of texts. This is rather different from the usual form of dialogue where one character puts forward a fragment of a discourse to which a second character then responds.
Our method requires a more complex reading of the geometry of these texts carried by several narrators simultaneously. Geometry is a way of connecting fragments while allowing them to retain their own coherence, without mashing them into one 'coherent' story. Also, in this play, we take texts that are supposed to be traditional and give them a modern interpretation. New meanings have to be found because otherwise you are left only with sentimental meanings. Geometry is opposed to nostalgia. Nostalgia takes fragments which are dispersed in real existence and wraps them up in a neatly packaged narrative to deliver them to the souvenir shop.

I want to relate the geometry of the texts to the geography of Venice, which is a very complicated city to penetrate. It has a very delicate yet overwhelming existence. It is not really a ruin since it has already integrated the notion that it is a touristic ruin. It has already been interpreted by Thomas Mann and by many others. If you try to integrate Venice with its sophisticated architectural identity into your play, you risk finding a very evanescent entity. When you insert a visual presentation into a place, you have to understand the parameters of your action, because the place will start interacting, conversing with you.

At first, two places seemed very interesting for my purposes. The first was the island of San Giorgio. I wanted to use the water to work on reflections. With Henri Alekan, we considered putting very large mirrors in the water and to project light onto them. As the stage, there would be a linear configuration in the water so that the spectacle would be organised like a procession. That would connect the text with the destruction of Jerusalem and the temple and also with the beginning of the diaspora. Jewish slaves were brought to Rome to parade in a procession and eventually they fanned out all over Europe and beyond, creating Jewish communities.

The second place was the ghetto. The ghetto of Venice was the first one ever established. In fact, the word ghetto comes from Venice. In 1516, the pope allowed the Jews to come to Venice on condition that they would settle in a particular, restricted compound. So there is a historical bridge between a text about the destruction of one city, Jerusalem, and the formation of the first exclusion zone in another city, the ghetto of Venice, fifteen hundred years later.

In the end, I decided to do something very abstract and to use a form which recurs in many paintings: the last supper. When you look at the fresco by Andrea Del Castagno at Sant' Apollonia in Florence, you find that harsh horizontal presence of the table: a straight, white surface cuts through the figures. This spatial organisation is also a classic image of the 20th century: people sit behind tables like that with microphones and glasses of water for press conferences. The good thing about such a layout is that I can strip the text of any 'enactment' dimension and work basically with its recitative qualities. The epic narrators behind the table will use several different languages: Yiddish, Hebrew, German, French, American, Arabic, Italian. The table, an archaic, minimal form of a stage, will unify the tale visually.

This also gives me an opportunity to present the tensions between a variety of languages and their historical contexts in a contemporary formation. I am very interested in those kinds of non-correlations. Hebrew is a helpful language in that sense. It is a minority language, so that gives it a kind of distance. And it is a very chopped, staccato language, not very descriptive. In our modern interpretation of the text of Flavius Josephus, we keep a variety of languages, accents, intonations and so on, and we present the tensions between them. These tensions are a sign of twentieth century culture: people migrate across the surface of the earth and when they settle somewhere, they express themselves in an often broken but unique manner. We need to create a dialogue with all those ingredients and we also have to consider the ethics of using 'ingredients' taken from outside our own cultures: to what extent are these ingredients available to us? Is there a limit to using them? Do we have to label them when we remove them from their original context?

In his introduction, Flavius Josephus mentions that he originally wrote *The Jewish War* in Hebrew and that he translated it into Greek to reach a wider audience, to let other people share his knowledge. But the original Hebrew version has never been found. So we are dealing with an already translated text. I am sceptical about translations because you lose a lot, like the sonorous qualities of the language. Besides, texts may be stripped of some important ambiguities. The famous St James version of the *Bible* always selected the divine interpretation of things that were more ambiguous in Hebrew. In Hebrew, the word for 'heaven' is the same as that for 'sky'. The English version always chooses the metaphysical 'heaven', never the physical 'sky'. In *Genesis,* for example, you cannot really follow the descriptive dimension of god's actions. In Hebrew, he acts like a painter who divides up a surface. In the original text, you can imagine him in front of a canvas, outlining the surfaces he wants to work with: water over here, sky over there. Moreover, the Biblical writer integrated the sound of the language into the description. The Hebrew word for water is 'maïm' and the word for 'sky' or 'heaven' is 'shamaïm', meaning 'there water'. So, you can visualize somebody tracing a line on a canvas and deciding that water shall be 'there'. You do not get that in the English translation.

As a procedure, I feel comfortable with the juxtaposition of different languages. I like having, say, a passage in English, which has the aura of an imperial language, and to have another actor speak the translation into a local language afterwards. English is the language of computers, of the stock exchange, of rock music. It has become a kind of bastard language of modernity, stripped of certain literary qualities but really functional.

The text we used in Gibellina relates to this kind of modernity. You can relate it, for instance, to the current situation in Eastern Europe: the Massada story is about suicide and extermination. If you have an intelligent audience as a partner, an audience prepared to bring an active attention to the film or the play, you do not need to be totally explicit or too direct.

Someone asked George Steiner once what it meant to be a Jew in the 20th century. He replied: 'I teach my children that there are two important lessons about being a Jew: one should learn many languages and one should be able to pack one's bags very quickly.

Bernard Hébert

Amos Gitai

PART IV

ALEKAN ON GITAI

Amos Gitai called on Henri Alekan's expertise in 1985 for his first feature film, *Esther,* and they continued working together on *Berlin-Jerusalem* (1988) and *Golem: L'Esprit de l'Exil* (1991). The following interview was conducted by Stephan Levine shortly after Gitai and Alekan had completed the trilogy.

Stephan Levine: *How do you go about choosing a visual style for your collaboration with Amos Gitai?*

Henri Alekan: For *Berlin-Jerusalem* we wanted something close to the style of expressionist painters such as Grozs or Otto Dix. I think that era is extremely important in the history of painting: the movement of German painters between 1918 and the rise of fascism. They wanted to get away from the middle-class mentality and to find new forms of expression closer to the people. The fascists regarded it as a degraded, decadent form of painting. There were some wonderful films in the cinema of that period : *The Threepenny Opera, M.* As for me, I was probably very influenced by my meetings with Eugen Schüfftan, the great cinematographer who worked with Ophuls and Pabst when they came to make films in France, and by the private conversations I had with those directors at the time.

SL: *When you recreated 30s Berlin with Amos Gitai for* Berlin-Jerusalem, *were you consciously referring to those memories?*

HA: While you are working you don't analyse everything that passes through your mind, but I believe that influences come to the surface when you have to create something. I call them memorial images: all of a sudden they re-emerge and they can help you to create a certain photographic atmosphere. You never invent things from nothing. There is no such thing as pure invention: we are made up of an accumulation of images stored in our memory. I never lived in 30s Germany but I experienced that period in the way people talked about it; also

Berlin Jerusalem

through photographs, through the work of German expressionist painters and directors, and some of the images left a deep impression and have stayed with me. I was also influenced by the theatre of that time which brought something radically new to the *mise en scène* and the lighting. I had the good fortune of experiencing that period very intensely and I accumulated observations and images without knowing that they would come in handy later. All those memories strongly influenced my work of reconstruction with Amos Gitai for *Berlin-Jerusalem*. The idea of reconstructing Berlin through expressionist lighting effects interested me very much.

SL: *Besides your memories and references, your work is also marked by your wide-ranging technical knowledge. On the main set of* Berlin-Jerusalem *– a gigantic loft transformed into a studio – there were iron pillars, a big staircase... How did the lighting actually work, concretely, in that structure?*

HA: There is indeed that whole material aspect. Lighting means projectors... You are constantly confronted with concrete things, the *real-isation*, and you must know how to come to grips with that. I like to remind my students that you also must be a bit of an electrician. You must have touched projectors to know they are burning hot and that you must wear gloves, that they are heavy, etc. Of course, you have to go beyond the abstract concept and translate it into a specific lighting plan. I can't say that all my work is premeditated, only part of it. Most of my work is done actually dealing with the concrete, materiality of volumes and the forms. Many things are found on the spot. Amos comes from architecture and you can sense it in the way he prepares the framings. He always wants to *architecturise* the image in terms of the design and the forms presented in the field of vision. Some work differently. For instance, Julien Duvivier insisted that everything should be written down in advance – which results in a very rigid *mise en scène*. In his scripts, he marked in advance each camera placement, the lens to be used, the movements to be made, etc. The people around him merely carried out the instructions. It was an entirely premeditated mise en scène. For the light, I could take all the time I needed.

SL: *How did you make the change from that way of shooting to films such as those of Amos Gitai where the actual shooting conditions play a role and force you to find quick solutions?*

HA: I try to adapt myself to the director's way of doing things. Amos's method has nothing in common with Duvivier's. He comes with an overall idea, but in the face of concrete reality, in the face of the reality of the places and the forms, he transforms his *mise en scène*. And he leaves me great freedom for the lighting. The work is carried out in a flexible manner. I also worked with Wim Wenders and his working method was similar.

SL: *Do you always achieve the result you want?*

HA: I was very unhappy when we shot the marriage procession by the banks of the Seine for *L'Esprit de l'Exil*. There was a splendid winter sun and they all went on doing their job oblivious to the reality of the situation: that the sun would soon disappear... But Amos wasn't bothered by that. What he wanted was a perfect camera movement fitting in with the architecture of the whole sequence, even at the risk of losing something of the special sunlight. When shooting, it is the director who defines the overall balance in his film. The essential thing is to have continuity you carry within yourself.

SL: *How does it take shape? In conversation with the director or in your own reflections as you go along?*

HA: It's a mixture of the two. There are the conversations but you also bring some very personal concept to bear as well. You have to try and align your personal concept with that of the director, to achieve what he is looking for. With Amos, I sense, I propose, I show what I can do. When we shot the meal scene inside (the scene of the first meeting with Boaz in *L'Esprit de l'Exil*) I wanted a composition inspired by Italian painting, with high contrasts. I was thinking of Da Vinci's *Last Supper*. As soon as we arrived on the set I knew how I wanted the table to be lit, with slightly effaced backgrounds.

SL: Esther *was your first film with Amos Gitai. What attracted you to the project?*

102

Bernard Hebert

Berlin-Jerusalem

HA: Amos had shown me two of his documentaries, *Pineapple* and *House*, and I found them very interesting. Not at all banal. And then, I was attracted to the idea of going to Israel. I had never been there because, although I am of Jewish origins, I don't bother about religion. And it seemed to me that Israel was a country where religion dominated everything: politics, the economy ...

I really loved participating in the location hunts for *Esther*. The film had been conceived in such a way that we didn't need to find historically realistic decors. The viewer was to be given the opportunity to interpret the settings in terms of the sequence shots and the way the scenes followed each other. There was a theatrical aspect to the way the images were conceived and the locations suited that very well.

SL: *The film transposes the story of Esther to the ruins of an Arab quarter in Haifa. When you work with Amos Gitai, do you have the impression that you are taking part in political films?*

HA: Yes, there are political undertones in each one of them. The shoot itself had a political meaning. Contrary to what I had imagined, everything went very well between the Israeli technicians and the Palestinian actors who were part of the cast. I asked myself: how come there are so many problems in this country between Jews and Arabs when, in practice, people can understand and get on with each other; why then should it be impossible to get on and to arrive at some agreement at a higher level? Therefore the problem struck me as not a real one.

SL: *In Israel, the sun's luminosity is very strong, very direct. Did the exterior scenes cause you any particular difficulties?*

HA: Yes, it was difficult because the intense sunlight creates shadows that can often be too hard and go against the overall aesthetic. The actors were very beautiful, very interesting to light. I am particularly sensitive to the beauty of men and women, to the beauty of the body and of the face. That doesn't mean I am looking for classical perfection, but there is real joy in finding the light that suits the morphology of a face, on this or that type of skin. You must also take care not to devise a light that would go against an actor's expression at a given moment. So you try to place the characters counter to the sun or to re-light them with reflecting screens to soften the shadows or to filter the sun with gauzes when that is possible. We insisted on modulating the light intensities and all those modulations are shown in continuity, in sequence shots.

SL: *Those sequence shots are an integral part of the film's conception, as they are in* Berlin-Jerusalem *and in the film you just shot last autumn with Amos Gitai,* L'Esprit de l'Exil.

HA: That's one of the challenges of working with Amos. Shooting in sequence shots sometimes prevents you from placing the projectors or the reflectors where you want them. But the advantage is that the film shows the whole substance and the whole process in one go, without cutting up the scenes, hacking them up. The system of cutting the film into little pieces – inserting detail shots – was a style practiced at one time, but I think in today's cinema this is being re-thought. More often people try to capture the atmosphere of a scene in its continuity. I think it corresponds to the look of the viewer who thus becomes complicit with the actors. This fluidity allows for a real visual and sound continuity without editing artifices. In the sequence shot, it is a little as if the viewer were walking alongside the actors, next to them, behind them, with our own way of looking. Our look doesn't make cuts, it is continuous. Amos creates that will towards continuity in all his films.

SL: *Does that imply a different way of lighting?*

HA: For the lighting cameraman, it isn't easy. You can't assume that it will be possible to adjust the placement of the projectors during the scene. You have to put the projectors in their definitive place right from the outset. The flow of light has to be organised once and for all. Or you have to take into account the movement of the sun throughout the shot.

On Esther, some things had been decided in advance, on the basis of the script, but a great deal had to be adapted on the spot, which sometimes allows you to find a better solution than classic lighting patterns. There was a mixture of real-life decors and decors arranged for the scenes. Let me give you an example: for one scene, in the Royal Palace, the lighting had been worked out well in advance. In such a case, you have to know whether you want to retain a kind of realism for the scene, for the characters, or whether you can transpose things. We chose to do a transposition. There is nothing natural in the lighting of that scene. For the operator, the difficulty in a real interior is that you can't place the light sources where you want them. There is constant to and fro between what you hope for and what you get, between what you want, what you imagine, and the reality, which means that the projectors are not always where you want them.

SL: *Your lighting is never unilateral. You play with dark surfaces and intricately arranged spots of light.*

HA: For the hanging of Haman in *Esther,* the image was constructed in terms of very high contrasts between a strongly sunlit area and squares of shadows. It was a composition close to that of a painter. The direction had a very elaborate geometry and the lighting followed suit. This requires close collaboration with the director. In that particular case, the sun was largely responsible for the light, but the image composition was not left to chance: Amos wanted those relations between light and shadow. If we had shot at five o'clock in the evening, the result would have been quite different.

You have to put into play as much as possible the oppositions between bright surfaces and dark ones. Of course, when everything is white you still have an image, and when everything is dark you also still have an image, but you don't have the *music* of the light. I mean, you don't have light modulations, comparable to the modulations in the tonal scale. Bright ones, less bright ones, greys, less grey ones, greyer ones, transparent blacks, dark blacks... A whole range of light-values which play on the viewer's perception. The viewer is sensitive to those variations of light and shade, just like in music. You musn't content yourself with uniform lighting pattern, with the same density or the same intensity, but try – artificially with projectors or by playing with solar light – to provide a vast range of light values.

SL: *Is there something that remained constant throughout your work on the trilogy of* Esther, Berlin-Jerusalem *and* L'Esprit de l'Exil?

HA: Looking at them again, no doubt one could find family resemblances. To my mind, the same rules always apply but I try to put them into brackets, not to use systematically the same lighting principles. Sometimes, those principles intervene in spite of myself, but I try to create a different lighting pattern for each film.

SL: *Which makes you an ideal partner of a contemporary director, whereas one might have imagined you to be a very traditionalist and classical cinematographer.*

HA: I believe that at the time of the New Wave, directors were mistaken about me when they assumed that I was unable to free myself from my classical past. That was due to ignorance because they didn't know me nor the films I had made. All they had to do was look at them to see that I changed the lighting according to whether it was a comedy, *La Belle et la bête* or a crime film. The directors of that period had made a very categorical judgment about me.

Henri Alekan on the set of *Esther*

Amos Gitai

PART V

BIO-FILMOGRAPHY

Amos Gitai was born in Haifa on 11 October 1950. His father, Munio Weinraub-Gitai, born in Poland in 1909, studied at the Bauhaus (Dessau) and worked with Mies van der Rohe in Berlin until he was arrested by the Nazis in 1933. After a painful incarceration, he was released and escaped to the Swiss mountains until the Swiss authorities started returning illegal immigrants back to Germany. Munio Weinraub then caught a boat to Palestine in 1933. He taught architecture to building workers in Haifa and was responsible for a variety of public buildings, including schools, theatres, kibbutzim and also for urban planning in Haifa and Tel Aviv. Gitai's maternal grandparents, Eliyahu and Esther Munchick Margalit, of Russian origin, emigrated to Palestine around 1900 and participated in the foundation of the early kibbutz and trade union movements.

From 1971 to 1975 Amos Gitai studied architecture at Haifa's Technion and started making his first experimental films in Super-8. In 1973, during the Yom Kippur War, he served in an airborne ambulance unit. His helicopter was shot down by the Syrians (see *Ahare,* 1974). In 1976 he won an opportunity to study at the University of California at Berkeley, where in 1986 he was awarded a doctorate in architecture with a thesis on the architecture of five urban Jewish communities. In 1977 he worked for Israeli Television, making many programmes and documentaries, the last of which, entitled *Bait (House),* was not transmitted on account of its sympathetic attitude towards Palestinians. When it was screened privately and to kibbutzim, it aroused much controversy, prompting Gitai to take film-making seriously. While continuing to study architecture, he made several films, among them *Field Diary* (1982), which was shown at a number of film festivals and broadcast throughout Europe earning him an international reputation. For a long time the film was not shown in Israel due to its explicit antimilitarism.

After several documentaries shot in different parts of the world, Gitai made his first fiction feature in 1985, *Esther,* and continued exploring the motifs of exile and migration in his next two features, *Berlin-Jerusalem* and *Golem – L'Esprit de l'Exil*, the latter film of the trilogy simultaneously initiating a series of further explorations of the Golem theme. In 1991, he returned to the Wadi Rushmia in Haifa and updated his 1980 film, so that the new version, *Wadi* 1981-1991, in effect provided a chronicle of the way a decade of Israeli history affected people's lives. In 1992, he staged a play in Gibellina in Sicily and in 1993 he directed the theatrical performance which opened the Venice Biennale, both addressing key aspects of Jewish history via Flavius Josephus' epic *The Jewish War*. At the same time, Gitai shot a feature film in Leningrad while that city was turning into Petersburg and a documentary in Wupperthal in the days immediately after a gruesome, anti-semitic murder. In 1985 the British Film Institute in London devoted a retrospective to his films, followed by similar tributes in Frankfurt, Paris and Sidney (1986), Montpellier and Jerusalem (1987), Madrid and Strasburg (1988), Rotterdam, New York, Washington, Chicago (1989), Montreal (1990), Toronto and Moscow (1991), Turin, London and Warsaw (1992).

ANNOTATED FILMOGRAPHY

ARTS AND CRAFTS AND TECHNOLOGY
Israel 1973; super-8; col; 9 mins.
d Amos Gitai

A super-8 film about the various building traditions in Israel made in Haifa while studying architecture. It was shown, together with *Details of Architecture*, in Milan at a festival of industrial design in 1973. The catalogue listed them under the single, somewhat eccentric title, *Hebron Blow Glass*, attributed to a Mr Gihai.

DETAILS OF ARCHITECTURE
Israel 1973; super-8; col; 9 mins.
d Amos Gitai

'A film about modern architecture in Israel. It starts from the so-called "romantic" architecture in the early part of the century developed by people who came from Germany and then went to study Islamic architecture in Turkey. It was very eclectic and used old materials like Nubian sandstone, with many arches and architraves and so on. Then there was a brief neoclassical period coming from Europe and towards the end of the 1930s a strong influence of the Bauhaus began imposing itself, lasting until the end of the 1950s. Since 1967 a taste developed for massive, bunker-style edifices. It is still there today. But the origins of that style go back a long way, perhaps to the crusade.' (AG)

MEDABRIN AL ECOLOGIA
aka TALKING ABOUT ECOLOGY
Israel 1973; 16mm; col; 11 mins.
d Amos Gitai

'It simply shows the various positions expressed at a seminar on ecology in Haifa. Haifa is the centre of heavy industry and of the chemical industries as well as being a big port. So the city was the first to experience problems of pollution.' (AG)

MEMPHIS
Israel 1974; super-8; col; 7 mins.
d Amos Gitai

'This was shot driving through the black ghetto in Memphis. It's just people in the streets. I was interested in how people behaved when they look at the camera and see themselves being filmed. Like all my early films, it was edited in the camera while shooting.' (AG)

GALIM
aka WAVES
Israel 1974; super-8; col; 4 mins.
d Amos Gitai

An experimental film showing only waves of the Mediterranean.

AHARE
aka AFTER
Israel 1974; 16 mm; col; 13 mins.
d/c Amos Gitai ed David Tor, Yitzak Tzhaiek *pc* Israeli Film Centre

'A very personal story and also the first film for which I received a subsidy from the Israeli Film Centre. Actually, the grant was for another film on architecture but then the 1973 war happened and like many others in Israel I was drafted. I was part of a unit that had to transport the wounded back to a hospital with a Red Cross helicopter. On one of those operations the Syrians shot down the helicopter and one of the pilots was killed in a gruesome manner. We flew on for a couple of hours, with one pilot dead and the other wounded, before crashing. I was the only one to come out uninjured but for six months afterwards I remained dazed. I had to come to terms with the fact that I was alive while all the others had died. I then went back to the area were we had been hit and made the film. Usually I carried my super-8 camera with me but on that occasion we had left in a great hurry in response to an alarm and it was the only time I didn't take it. Just as well, really, since it would have been destroyed. So I went back and filmed all the objects I had left behind. The film itself is like one of those objects people bring back from the war as a kind of memento. A lot of work went into it; it was very carefully and elaborately edited. I did the music myself using sounds produced with equipment belonging to the architecture faculty's acoustics department which was normally used to test various architectural materials and to study types of sound proofing.' (AG)

CHARISMA
Israel 1976; 16 mm; col; 20 mins.
d/c Amos Gitai pc Israeli Film Centre mus Folk Songs by Luciano Berio sung by Cathy Berberian ed Rina Ben Melech lp Adina Baron

'The film combines a poem by Brecht with a documentary situation. A friend of mine, Adina Baron, a body artist, used to do performances in museums, exhibiting herself doing a kind of conceptual dance. It was like filming a sculpture accompanied by the words of Brecht's poem, *A Worker Reads History*. It is a very realist, militant poem whereas the film isn't realist at all but rather something which moves between an abstract form and a concrete situation. It was shot in an urban part of Haifa, in one of those Wadis where I later made other films.' (AG)

DIMITRI
Israel 1977; 16 mm; b/w; 18 mins.
d Amos Gitai pc Israeli TV

A documentary for children's TV about the clown Dimitri, shot in Versio near Ticino in Switzerland. The theme is similar to that of *Charisma*, mainly moving between the performance rhythms of the theatrical stage and the casual rhythms of everyday life.

HAGVUL
aka THE FRONTIER
Israel 1977; 16 mm; b/w; 15 mins.
d Amos Gitai pc Israeli TV

'This was the time when Israel was very proud of its Barlev Line, a series of fortifications along the Suez Canal. So I went to France, to the old Maginot Line, and spoke with the young farmers living there to find out how they related to these old military structures next to which they were working the land. I wanted to find out what it meant when people begin to put their trust only into fortifications.' (AG)

SHIRIM BE AFULA
aka SINGING IN AFULA
Israel 1977; 16 mm; b/w; 15 mins.
d Amos Gitai pc Israeli TV
A singing contest for children in a little provincial town near Nazareth.

POLITICAL MYTHS
Israel 1977; 16 mm; b/w; 30 mins.
d Amos Gitai

This film was shown for a while under the title *Charisma* but the title was changed to avoid confusion with AG's previous film called *Charisma*.

YGAL TOMARKIN: Gitai reminds me of long-forgotten memories, things I didn't know still existed. In my youth, I saw Polish revisionists in brown saluting with raised arms, admiring Jabotinsky and, no less, Mussolini. Since then, I have also seen the 'worker platoons' who admired Aba Chushi [former mayor of Haifa]. Red Haifa was not less fascist – less veneration and more of the red stuff, also more efficient. Since the decline of the youth movement, I tended to believe that the only uniformed people left were the 'chassidim' in the courts of their admired rabbis. Still, here they are! A group of Betar [youth movement of the right Herut party] youth leaders in brown uniforms with their shouts of 'Tel Chai'. Small Beta members jumping through burning hoops like lions in a circus. A chap who looks like an ape, with glasses, explains with the utmost seriousness: 'Here we construct the excellent Israeli race, the proud, intelligent, decisive Jew, the one who aspires to the frontiers between the great rivers and the Nile.' Modestly, he might be satisfied with the Suez Canal, even though it is not a natural river. And here, in Massada, are the tiny black Betar members. A youth leader wearing a skull cap reads the words of Elazar ben Yair. God's words are alive. One commits suicide and dies: 'There is nothing more beautiful and wonderful than to die for one's country, and in Massada they killed themselves to anger the Romans.' Israel in the late 70s. Pay attention. Such a film should not be banned. It should be shown every day as a public warning. (*Ha'ir,* Tel Aviv, 1 January, 1982.)

Amos Gitai has been banned twice by television. In both cases, it was the [Israeli] TV network which commissioned the films. Gitai has a clear visual language, even a personal one: this includes choice of subject, composition and editorial continuity. He does not use running commentary. This emerges from the filmed events – and so it should. In Gitai's black and white I did not miss colour. In the same way, his messages fit in with the pictures and the speech rhythms. (*Kol Ha'ir,* Jerusalem, 2 October, 1981.)

SHIKUN
aka PUBLIC HOUSE
Israel 1977; 16mm; b/w; 23 mins.

d Amos Gitai *pc* Israeli TV
Description of the construction of a building.

BETOCH HAMAIN
aka UNDER THE WATER
Israel 1977; 16 mm; *b/w*; 18 mins.

d Amos Gitai *pc* Israeli TV
An experiment in underwater shooting in the Red Sea near Elat.

ARCHITECTURA
Israel 1978; 16 mm; *b/w*; 39 mins.
d Amos Gitai *pc* Israeli TV

'This is my last film about architecture. It also consists of a series of capsule shots looking at different architectural traditions. One is about the local, vernacular style of building, the other about the more institutional, international style. The film confronts these two styles through sequences shot in various parts of the country.' (AG)

WADI RUSHMIA
Israel 1978; 16 mm; b/w; 36 mins.
d Amos Gitai *pc* Israeli TV

Reportage shot in the Wadi Rushmia valley in Haifa. It shows the Arab and Jewish families living there while the Municipal authorities attempt to 'rehabilitate' the area. One of the questions raised is that of options facing municipalities when deciding to impose a particular urban environment or to allow its people who live in the affected areas to create their own environment.

MEORAOT WADI SALIB
aka WADI SALIB RIOTS
Israel 1979; 16 mm; b/w; 40 mins.
d Amos Gitai *pc* Israeli TV *c* Yacov Saporta *sd* Yitzak Cohen

'Salib is one of the Wadis in Haifa. Before 1948, it was inhabited mainly by Palestinians. After the war, the area was evacuated and Jews from North Africa were settled there. In 1959, the African Jews rebelled against the snobbery of the Labour Party which treated them as inferior people. There was trouble throughout the country and in Salib they set fire to part of the area. In a way, the current political patterns, with many North African Jews voting for the right, were produced at that time.
   It is a Brechtian kind of story, a sort of *Threepenny Opera*. The protagonists are three heroes of the rebellion. One was a Mack The Knife figure, half gangster and half political leader. He made an alliance with a guy who owned a little bar, and the third one was the ideologue, a Maoist making official pronouncements. When these three got together, it resulted in the destruction of the area. The army, with Dayan in charge, surrounded the Wadi and the area was destroyed. Its people were dispersed throughout the city. Each of the three is treated differently: the ideologue has his head smashed in and his body is thrown away, the bar owner gets a bigger bar and the third one remains a "stray dog". It's a real melodrama, a kind of musical. Someday it should be made as a fiction film. Mack (his real name was Josef) wound up in prison and during his trial, a journalist of German origin, a member of the Communist Party, fell in love with him. It's a real film story, very kitsch.
   The film constantly goes from the historical characters to what they have become today. Instead of bringing them together in a studio, I went to find them where they are living now. For instance, I had to go to the Red Sea to find the guy with the restaurant and to make him talk about the events of 1959.' (AG)

CULTURAL CELEBRITIES
Israel 1979; video, col; 50 mins.
d/p/c Amos Gitai *pc* Capital Studios (Jerusalem) *sd* Joshua Reichek *ed* Dick Lindheim *lp* Jane Fonda, Francis F. Coppola, Barry Scott, Betsey Johnson, Philip Johnson

'This was a kind of model for the two parts of *American Mythologies* I made later. It was research on notions of style, on the architecture and the images of the 1970: postmodern architecture, Jane Fonda and Berkeley, the black ghetto, the anti-nuclear movements, punk fashion design with the swastikas taken from Hollywood...' (AG)

BIKUR CARTER BE'ISRAEL
aka CARTER'S VISIT TO ISRAEL
Israel 1979; 16 mm; b/w; 12 mins.
d Amos Gitai *pc* Israeli TV

'A reportage commissioned by television when the president of the USA visited Israel. *Wadi Rushmia* had been very well received and so they commissioned me for this job, which I really didn't want to do at all. That's why I did things like putting very pompous orchestral music on the soundtrack, at other times using the actual sound. I simply changed the sounds because it was finished only at the last minute and they had no chance of seeing it before the broadcast. The official reporter was extremely upset, insisting that the sound should only ever illustrate the situation. Instead, there was this pompous orchestral stuff while the ministers were waiting for the president's plane to land. It was rather comical.' (AG)

BAIT
aka HOUSE
Israel 1980; 16 mm; b/w; 51 mins.
d Amos Gitai *pc* Israeli TV *c* Emanuel Aldema *ed* Rina Ben Melech
sd Oded Hornik

ANNE KIEFFER: In a quarry near Mount Hebron workers extract blocks of stone to be used to rebuild a house on the West Bank. Amos Gitai investigates the memory of that house and sets out to find its different occupants. In 1948 it belonged to a Palestinian, Mahmoud Djana; in 1967, with the occupation, it became the property of the state of Israel which rented it out to Algerian Jews and, a few years later, sold it to an Israeli professor, Chaim Barka. This journey into the past occurs while the house is being re-developed. To trace the history of a house naturally leads to tracing the history of the land. Amos Gitai adds his own look at the current building works. All the labourers are Palestinian, hired by an Iraqi-Jewish developer, Ben Menastre. Most of them come from villages occupied by the Jews since 1948. One of them says 'I detest them all as much as they detest me. I work here from six in the morning to ten at night for 550 Israeli pounds. If all the Arab governments couldn't stop Israel, how could we?' *House* begins and ends with the same shot: the quarry near Mount Hebron where other pieces of rock are being excavated to build more houses. One worker kneels and prays, facing the Holy City. The circle closes on the jagged fissures of a broken rock, leaving the marks of a resistance. ('Upon this rock...' in *Afrique-Asie*, 24 May. 1982.)

WADI
Israel 1980; 16 mm; col; 40 mins.
d/p Amos Gitai *c* Yakov Saporta, Yosi Wein *sd* Yitzak Cohen, Eli Yarkoni
mus 'Thorns' by The National Gathering *ed* Solveig Nordlund
lp Aisha, Yussuf, Iso, Salo, Myriam, Iskander

Documentary shot in the Wadi Rushia in Haifa. This film later became the first part of *Wadi* 1981-1991.

IN SEARCH OF IDENTITY
Israel 1980; 16mm; col; 57 mins.
d Amos Gitai *pc* Slonim (Tel Aviv) *c* Yakov Saporta *sd* Shabtai Sarig
lp Saul Bellow, I. F. Stone, A. Farbstein et al.

I.F. Stone in *In Search of Identity*

'The film of a journey to the USA to do a series of interviews with American Jews: Saul Bellow, I. F Stone, A. Farbstein, who was Trostky's secretary, the Levi Strauss family (the Jeans one) and at the beginning, a woman from a small Colorado village I came across as she went to the sheriff demanding to know whether there were any Jews in the area. Of course, he immediately pointed to one right there.

The theme of the interviews is identity: how can you identify yourself as a Jew, the question of roots, typical problems of countries inhabited by immigrants like the US when compared to Israel. The title is important. Searching for identity is searching for something abstract, very difficult to define. Historically, when the severe discrimination against the Jews came to an end in the 19th century, with the Code Napoleon, the opening of the ghettoes, and so on, the sense of identity which was so strong during the oppression became much more problematic. Israel itself is part of that search, a kind of reaction to the crumbling of the ghetto walls which produced the building of other walls, the borders of a State.' (AG)

AMERICAN MYTHOLOGIES
PART I: Rituals ; PART II: Elsewhere
Israel/Finland 1981; 16 mm; col; 104 mins. (2 x 52 mins)
d/p Amos Gitai *pc* Epidem/Amos Gitai Prods *c* Valery Galprin, Yakov Saporta
sd Eugene Lynch, Udi Eghoise *ed* Yussa Salminem
lp Francis F. Coppola, Jane Fonda, Betsey Johnson, Paul Klein

A film about American culture when Reagan came to power in 1981, including conversations with Jane Fonda, Francis Ford Coppola, fashion designer Betsey Johnson, NBC's Head of Programming and various figures from the 'counter culture'. Amos Gitai also made a 52 minute version of the film called *Selling Time*.

FIELD DIARY
aka YOMAN SADE'
aka JOURNAL DE CAMPAGNE
Israel/ France 1982; 16mm; col; 83 mins.
d/p Amos Gitai *pc* Les Films d'Ici (Paris)/AG Productions (Tel Aviv) *c* Nurith Aviv
sd Thierry Delor, Saar Avigur, Chaim Mekelberg

A diary-format documentary shot in the occupied territories immediately before and during Israel's invasion of Lebanon.

ANANAS
aka PINEAPPLE
France 1984; 16 mm; col; 76 mins.
d/p Amos Gitai *pc* Les Films d'Ici (Paris)/ Amos Gitai Productions (Tel Aviv)/ FR3 (France)/ TV 2 (Finland)/ IKON (Netherlands)/ TVI (Sweden) *c* Nurith Aviv
sd Kevin Gallagher *ed* Juliana Sanchez

A documentary following a journey prompted by the markings on a tin of pineapple marketed by the Dole Pineapple Corporation.

BANGKOK BAHRAIN
aka LABOUR FOR SALE
France 1984; 16mm; col; 78 mins.
d/p Amos Gitai *pc* Amos Gitai Productions/TF1 (France)/Channel 4 (UK)/Ikon (Netherlands) *c* Roni Katzenelson, Richard Copans *ed* Juliana Sanchez
sd Olivier Schwob

An attempt to look at modern relationships between countries where the products to be sold and marketed are people who are hired and exported. Almost half-a-million women in Bangkok work as prostitutes driven into the cities by poverty and hunger in their villages, while the men are exported to the Gulf countries to work as cheap labourers in construction.

REAGAN: IMAGE FOR SALE
UK/FRANCE 1984; 16mm/Video; col; 60 mins.
d/p Amos Gitai *pc* Channel 4 (UK)/AGAV/IKON (Netherlands)

A documentary commissioned by Channel 4 in London for its *Eleventh Hour* programme. The film uses material shot but not used for *American Mythologies* (Philip Klein, Betsey Johnson, the model Patricia Pinkston, the reverend Robert Schuler, Francis Ford Coppola and others) together with newly shot material and ready-made television footage of the Republican convention in Dallas and other Republican propaganda materials. The theme is the manufacture and the selling of an image of Ronald Reagan. Amos Gitai commented: 'During the American elections of 1984 there was great enthusiasm for Reagan in England, so we tried to do something different. I asked for and obtained the rights to footage made by the Republican Party of its Dallas convention as well as its propaganda films. It was very interesting to see how the image of Ronald Reagan was constructed. Then I also re-used footage I had shot four years earlier for *American Mythologies* to show the relationship between the new American culture and its politics. For instance, the punk fashion designer, formerly with Andy Warhol's Velvet Underground, has a purely formalist relation with everything, including political events: she only sees its visual surface.'

ESTHER
Israel/UK 1986; 35mm; Fujicol; 97 mins.
d/p Amos Gitai *pc* Agav Films/ Channel Four(UK)/ ORF (Austria) / IKON (Netherlands) / United Studios Herzlia (Israel) *exec p* Ruben Korenfeld
sc Amos Gitai, Stephan Levine from the Biblical text *c* Henri Alekan
camera Nurith Aviv *p des* Richard Ingersoll *mus* Popular Jewish, Yemeni, Indian and Palestinian songs *ed* Sheherazad Saadi *costumes* Thierry Fortin
sd Claude Bertrand *sp.ef* Bachir Abou Rabia
lp Simona Benyamini *(Esther),* Mohammed Bakri *(Mordecai),* Julianno Merr *(Haman),* Zare Vartanian *(King Ahasverus),* Schmuel Wolf *(The Narrator),* David Cohen *(Hatak),* Sarah Cohen *(Singer in Hebrew),* Rim Bani *(Singer in Arabic)*

First 'fiction' feature faithfully retelling the *Old Testament* story of Esther.

BRAND NEW DAY
UK/France 1987; 35mm, col; 93 mins.
d/p Amos Gitai *pc* AGAV Films, Oil Factory (UK) *exec p* John Stewart *c* Nurith Aviv *ed* Anna Ruiz *mus* The Eurythmics *lp* Annie Lennox, David A. Stewart, Jimmy 'Z' Zavala, Patrick Seymour, Clem Burke, Chucho Mercham, Joniece Jamison, Ryuichi Sakamoto, Kenny Endo, Conny Plank, Toru Takemitsu, Watazumido Doso Roshi

'*Brand New Day* is a film about sonic space, about how a group of musicians, The Eurythmics, visited Japan while on a world tour connected with their 'Revenge' album. They go to a country with a sonic tradition of its own, passing through a mixture of modern, technological and traditional sounds. There are certain choices to be made. The musical sections are shot with a single camera, from a single reference point – unlike those concert films in which several cameras are used. And there are other choices: is the film going to be a video promo? Is it a concert film or a straight didactic documentary? We tried to avoid these equations and to make an associative piece. Each event, encounter, musical conversation becomes one element in an associative chain. Each element has its own sound – a factory, a concert, a conversation, the sound of the music materials of the film, a train, a bamboo forest, a buddhist ceremony. By the end of the film we are reminded of some of these in a sequence of sonic memories.' (AG)

  CLYDE JEAVONS: For his latest assignment, Amos Gitai's was to accompany Annie Lennox and Dave Stewart on the Eurythmics' visit to Japan

Annie Lennox in *Brand New Day*

Annie Lennox and Dave Stewart in *Brand New Day*

during their world tour and record their impressions and encounters as well as their concerts. The result is a fascinating and idiosyncratic exploration of Japan and its music culture, during which taciturn Dave and the more talkative Annie improvise and philosophise respectively, experiment with Japanese sounds and locations, compare notes (in every sense) with local musicians, and reveal to the full their genuine passion for music and gift for live performance, be it in concert, bamboo forest or the backs of cars. Gitai's reflective, low-key, intelligent, sometimes tongue-in-cheek approach, moreover, combined with a new-found eye for composition to complement Nurith Aviv's striking photography, considerably raises the tone of this kind of rock-doc material, which in flashier but crasser hands normally ends up being simply raucous and moribund.

BERLIN-JERUSALEM
France/Israel/UK/Italy/Netherlands1989; 35mm, col; 89 mins
d/p Amos Gitai *pc* AGAV Films/Channel 4 (UK)/La Sept, Maison de la Culture du Havre, CNC (France)/Nova Films, RAI 2 (Italy)/Orthel Films, NOS, Hubert Bals Fund(Netherlands), Transfax (Israel) *sc* Amos Gitai, Gudie Lawaetz *c* Henri Alekan *mus* Markus Stockhausen *sd* Antoine Bonfanti *costumes* Gisela Storch *ed* Luc Barnier *ad* Marc Petit Jean, Emanuel Amrami *p mgr* Laurent Truchot *lp* Lisa Kreuzer *(Else),* Rivka Neuman *(Tania),* Markus Stockhausen *(Ludwig),* Benjamin Levy *(Paul, Else's son),* Vernon Dobtcheff *(Editor in Berlin),* Veronica Lazare *(Cassandra, his secretary),* Bernard Eisenschitz *(Man in Berlin café),* Raoul Guylad *(Dr. Weintraub),* Christian Van Acken *(Ticket seller at Berlin train station),* Juliano Merr *(Menahem),* Ohad Shahar *(Nahum, Tania's brother),* Keren Mor *(Fania),* Bilha Rozenfeld *(Tzipora),* Dany Roth *(Yashek Levinski),* Gadi Por *(Nissanov),* Mark Ivanir *(Dov Ben Gelman),* Ori Levy *(Anton Keller),* Yossi Graber *(Zins)* and members of the Pina Bausch Dance Company

Feature film weaving together the journey of the poet Else Lasker-Schüler to Israel in the thirties with the story of the pioneering Zionist settlers from Russia, exemplified by a character inspired by the life of Mania Shohat.

Dominique Sanda in *Naissance d'un Golem*

NAISSANCE D'UN GOLEM
aka BIRTH OF A GOLEM
France 1991, Video, col, 60 mins
d/p/sc/ed Amos Gitai
pc AGAV Films *c* Henri Alekan, Nurith Aviv, Amos Gitai, Laurent Truchot *sd* Daniel Ollivier
lp Tonino Guerra, Dominique Sanda, Sapho, Annie Lennox, Henri Alekan, Adina Baron

A notebook exploring ideas for a feature on the theme of the Golem. In the process, the 'notebook' begins to take on a life of its own.

WADI 1981-1991
Israel/France/UK 1991, 16mm, col, 97 mins
d/p Amos Gitai *pc* AGAV Films, La Sept (France), Channel 4 Television (UK)
p mgr Laurent Truchot *c* Yakov Saporta, Yosi Wein (1981), Nurith Aviv (1991)
sd Yitzak Cohen, Eli Yarkoni (1981), Daniel Ollivier (1991) *ed* Solveig Nordlund (1981), Anna Ruiz (1991)
lp Yussuf, Aisha, Iso, Salo, Iskander, Myriam, Amar, Helene

A return visit, after a decade, to the people living in Haifa's Wadi Rushmia. The film consists of the 1980 film *Wadi* and new footage shot in 1991, including an extensive sequence at the Tel Aviv airport showing a new wave of East European immigrants. The new version was first broadcast in France by La Sept on January 8, 1992.

'Between 1981 and 1991 conditions in the valley have deteriorated quite a bit. The conflict between Arabs and Jews in this region created a great deal of tension between these people who try to hang on to their distinctive view of reality. Myriam and Iskander decided not to succumb to the cliches imposed by the dominant ideologies but in the end they fell victim to them. The large-scale conflict which destroys so many things destroyed even that fragile relationship. In fact, Wadi talks about a disappearing species because each camp wants to have disciplined soldiers at its disposal rather than people who break the nationalist straightjackets.' (AG)

GOLEM – L'ESPRIT DE L'EXIL
aka GOLEM – THE SPIRIT OF EXILE
France/Italy/Germany/Netherlands/UK 1992, 35mm, col, 105 mins
d/p/sc Amos Gitai *pc* AGAV Films, Groupe T.S.F., Canal + (France), Allarts (Amsterdam), Nova Films, Rai 2 (Rome), Friedlander Film Produktion (Hamburg), Channel 4 Television (London) *c* Henri Alekan *mus* Simon and Markus Stockhausen *sd* Antoine Bonfanti *ed* Anna Ruiz *p mgr* Laurent Truchot *costumes* Marie Vernoux, Jean-Pierre Delifer *ad* Thierry François
lp Hanna Schygulla *(The Spirit of Exile)*, Vittorio Mezzogiorno *(the Maharal)*, Ophrah Shemesh *(Naomi)*, Samuel Fuller *(Elimelek)*, Mireille Perrier *(Ruth)*, Sotigui Kouyaté *(Boaz)*, Fabienne Babe *(Orpa)*, Antonio Carallo *(Kylion)*, Bernard Levy *(Malhon)*, Bakary Sangare *(first sailor)*, Alain Maratrat *(second sailor)*, Marceline Loridan *(Orpa's mother)*, Bernardo Bertolucci *(Master of the Courtyard)*, Philippe Garrel *(Orpa's fiancé)*, Bernard Eisenschitz *(Daniel)*, Marisa Paredes, Fernand Moszkowicz and members of the Pina Bausch Dance Company

The Spirit of Exile refers to a dual mythology: one is the story of Ruth, taken from the Biblical text; this is interwoven with elements of the story of the Golem.

METAMORFOSI DI UNA MELODIA
aka METAMORPHOSIS OF A MELODY
Theatre performance in Gibellina (Sicily), July 1992.

d Amos Gitai pc AGAV Films, Comune di Gibellina, Télé Lyon Métropole, Université Catholique de Louvin, Nova texts Flavius Josephus's The Jewish War, Amos Gitai, Enrico Stassi, Roberto Andò, Rainer Maria Rilke, Oscar Wilde, the Bible, Hans Magnus Enzensberger adapted by Stephan Levine and Rivka Markovitzky Gitai mus Markus and Simon Stockhausen costumes Ophrah Shemesh lighting Enrico Bagnoli p mgrs Laurent Truchot, Eléonore Feneux lp Hanna Schygulla, Samuel Fuller, Enrico Lo Verso, Jerome Koenig, Ophrah Shemesh, Masha Itkina, Mariella Lo Sardo, Alberto Scala, Roberto Burgio, Paola Pace

Two videos were made of the performance: TITUS, a video record of the play supervised by Amos Gitai , shot by Peter Missoten, Yurgen Persun and Mathias Vanbuel, edited by Peter Missoten and recorded by Michel Boermans and Hans Helewant. The video was produced by the Université Catholique de Louvin. The second one is a video presenting a cinematic interpretation and impression of the event , VARIAZIONI SU 'METAMORFOSI DI UNA MELODIA'. It was directed by Daniele Cipri, Franco Maresco and Roberta Torre, produced by Agav Films (Paris) and Cinico Video (Palermo) and shot by Pierluigi Laffi and Marco Pipere.

DANS LA VALLEE DU WUPPER
aka IN THE VALLEY OF THE WUPPER
FRANCE 1993, 16mm, col, ca. 90 mins.
d/p/sc Amos Gitai pc AGAV Films, La Sept (France), Channel 4 Television (UK), RAI 3 (Rome) c Nurith Aviv, Max Rheinlander mus Simon Stockhausen sd Daniel Ollivier ed Eric Carlier

The place : the city of Wuppertal
The birthplace of Elsa Lasker-Schüler, the expressionist poet, friend of Franz Marc, Vassilly Kandinsky and Thomas Mann.
Her birthplace is at 150 meters from the BAYER factory: the producer of Aspirin and, during World War II, of the gas Cyclon B. The factory is at 180 meters from

the train station from which the Jews of the city were deported to extermination camps in Czechoslovakia and Poland. The station is at 200 meters from

the old jewish cemetery dating back to the beginning of the century. It was profaned several times in October and November of 1992. 100 meters from there

a school building serves as a refugee shelter for Muslims from the Kosovo region in Yugoslavia's war zone. On November 10, some youngsters entered the shelter armed with revolvers and fired shots to frighten the refugees. At 150 meters from there

a house protected by barbed wire and surveillance cameras. It is the local headquarters of the 'association for the defence of the purity of the German language', the non-official headquarters of some of the neo-nazi groups.
Wuppertal is a microcosm of recent events in Germany. It will be the focus for research into the social archaeology of these events.

We will tell our story through the events that took place on 13 November 1992 in a small bar in the city of Wuppertal, which is 40 km from Cologne.

The police said that two skinheads had confessed to murder. In a previously unreported case, the youths beat up, set ablaze and killed a 53 year-old butcher in the western part of Wuppertal because they thought he was a jew.

That murder, which took place on 13 November, came to light after the Dutch police told newspapers in the Netherlands that the murdered man's body had been driven across the border and dumped.

The victim, identified by the Dutch police as Karl Heinz Rohn, had been drinking in a Wuppertal bar when the skinheads, 18 and 24 year-old members of a neo-nazi group called the National Front, involved him in a political argument, prosecutors told the German news agency DPA.

After Mr Rohn reportedly called the skinheads 'nazi swine', the owner of the bar said 'He is a Jew!'.

Prosecutors said the skinheads then threw Mr Rohn off his stool, trampled him with their heavy boots, broke nearly all his ribs, doused him with schnapps and set fire to him. With the help of the bar-owner, the skinheads then dragged Mr Rohn into the bar-owner's car and drove Mr Rohn's body over the nearby border where they dumped him and left him to die.

German prosecutors said that Mr Rohn was not Jewish. An official at the Central Council of Jews in Germany said that the man had referred to himself as 'Half-Jewish'.

For the film-maker, the traveller in this place, reality is made up of the juxtaposition of different events registered in a number of places.

Else Lasker-Schüler, born in Elberfeld near Wuppertal, wrote the following poem in 1912:

There is lamentation in the world
As if God himself had died
The descending leaden cloud
is heavy with tombs
Life lies in every heart
as if in coffins
I want to return to infinity
into myself
Already the crocus of my heart
begins to blossom
perhaps it is already too late
oh, I am dying amongst you
I suffocate amongst you all
I want to wrap myself in threads
hanging in disarray
I am lost
And by losing you
I want to escape into myself.

LE JARDIN PETRIFIE
aka THE PETRIFIED GARDEN
France/Israel/Russia 1993,
35mm, col, 87 mins
d/p Amos Gitai *co-p* Gilles Sandouze *sc* Amos Gitai, Tonino Guerra *c* Henri Alekan, Eddie Timlin, Luc Drion *mus* Simon and Markus Stockhausen after a theme by Munio Weinraub-Gitai *ed* Anna Ruiz *p mgr* Laurent Truchot *lp* Hanna Schygulla, Jerome Koenig, Samuel Fuller, Masha Itkina, Arcadi Grayomoskeiekov, Yuri Klepikov, Natalia Silantyeva

The story of an art dealer who travels to post-USSR Russia in search of the Golem.

Le Jardin petrifié

THE WAR BETWEEN THE SONS OF LIGHT AND THE SONS OF DARKNESS
Theatre performance opening the Venice Biennale, June 1993. The text is derived mainly from the Dead Sea Scrolls and Flavius Josephus.